"Ben Conner achieves what few others have attempted. He informs both the head and the heart, calling church leaders and laypeople to be truly inclusive. This is a theological conversation of deep value for every reader — not just those interested in studies pertaining to disabilities. Conner's pastoral experience with teens with disabilities shines through, inviting churches to live into the theological claims they make."

— **Amy Jacober**
author of *The Adolescent Journey*

"Conner's book is not about how to fit adolescents into youth ministry but about how inclusive ministries with all kinds of adolescents, including those with developmental disabilities, embody the best of both missional and practical theologies. *Amplifying Our Witness* builds a framework of youth ministry that applies to anybody. . . . To use Conner's own words, inclusive youth ministries help adults to become more comfortable entering into the uncomfortable worlds of both adolescence and disability in ways that empower everyone."

— **Bill Gaventa**
director of Community and Congregational
Supports, Elizabeth M. Boggs Center
on Developmental Disabilities

"Far too many youth are missing out on the opportunity to journey in faith and friendship alongside their peers with developmental disabilities. Conner calls his readers to grasp a new vision for inclusive youth ministry — and he shows them how to get there. A compelling book."

— **Erik Carter**
author of *Including People with Disabilities
in Faith Communities*

AMPLIFYING OUR WITNESS

Giving Voice to Adolescents
with Developmental Disabilities

Benjamin T. Conner

WILLIAM B. EERDMANS PUBLISHING COMPANY
GRAND RAPIDS, MICHIGAN / CAMBRIDGE, U.K.

Published 2012 by
Wm. B. Eerdmans Publishing Co.
2140 Oak Industrial Drive N.E., Grand Rapids, Michigan 49505 /
P.O. Box 163, Cambridge CB3 9PU U.K.

Printed in the United States of America

18 17 16 15 14 13   7 6 5 4 3 2

Library of Congress Cataloging-in-Publication Data

Conner, Benjamin T.
    Amplifying our witness: giving voice to adolescents
    with developmental disabilities / Benjamin T. Conner.
        p.   cm.
    Includes bibliographical references (p.   ).
    ISBN 978-0-8028-6721-6 (pbk.)
    1. Church work with teenagers. 2. Church work with people
    with disabilities. I. Title.

    BV4447.C577 2011
    259'.23 — dc23

                                                    2011045360

www.eerdmans.com

Contents

Preface and Acknowledgments

I first imagined this book when I was writing my dissertation for Princeton Theological Seminary. I had just started a ministry to adolescents with developmental disabilities in Williamsburg, Virginia, and the practical lessons I was learning about communication, discipleship, and theology were posing a challenge to the way I had conceptualized and articulated my faith. When I completed my dissertation and was attempting to reconfigure and express it as a book proposal to Wm. B. Eerdmans *(Practicing Witness),* I decided I would also attach an extra paragraph about an idea I had for a book about ministry with adolescents with developmental disabilities. I was excited and edified to hear that Eerdmans was actually more interested in the second project.

Writing this book has been an exercise in practical theology, youth ministry, missiology, disability studies, and devotion. I have encountered the living Lord in so many ways — and I hope this is communicated through the stories. I have written what follows, but the content itself issues from a community that practices faith together and from a larger theological conversation, and I must recognize the contributors.

First, the young adults with whom I share ministry have been wonderful partners on this journey (the stories are all true, though their names have been changed). They have taught me how to teach and have led me into a holistic approach to Christian discipleship. I will call them the Thru the Roof Crew, and they know who they are. They may never read this book, but it would have been impossible to write without their contributions. I am also indebted to the many high school, college, and adult volunteers with whom I have partnered in this ministry. This includes my four children: Tommy, Tori, Taylor, and Tessa.

I thought first of calling the book *Amplifying Their Witness*. I was at the Institute on Theology and Disability at Lutheran Theological Seminary at Gettysburg preparing to present this book to those gathered when I decided to change the title. Sharing that time with so many people with a variety of disabilities, learning from and edifying one another, caused me to reevaluate the appropriateness of the title. At that conference there was no "their," only an "our." This, of course, is what this book is all about.

From the academic side, I greatly appreciate the input of the many people who have read drafts of this book and have given me feedback from a variety of disciplines. This includes, but is not limited to, Darrell Guder (missional theology), Amos Yong (disability studies and theology), Amy Julia Becker (blogger and author), Scott Swan (marketing), Lois Wright (social work), Craig Dykstra (practical theology), Hans Reinders (disability studies and ethics), John Swinton (practical theology and nursing), Bill Gaventa (disability studies), Kenda Dean (youth ministry), Erik Carter (special education), and Kelly Whalon (special education). Special thanks go to Taylor & Francis for permission to use extensively "Affirming Presence: Spiritual Life and Friendship with Adolescents with Developmental Disabilities" (http://www.informaworld.com).

Finally, I appreciate and recognize the input from pastors, friends, and family in the form of conversations and correspondences. I am especially grateful for the input and feedback from my wife, Melissa, who has been a lifelong partner in ministry.

BENJAMIN T. CONNER

chapter 1

Introduction

....

"Life Is Liturgy"

Disconnected

There is no way to enter a high school lunchroom as a forty-year-old without feeling like you are a visitor in a foreign culture. And you are. You don't understand how the spaces have been defined, you don't know the appropriate gestures or protocols for navigating the lunchroom, your clothing sets you apart as an outsider (especially the prominently placed "visitor" sticker), and the conversations have a rhythm and language to which you are not attuned. It is a loud, busy, and intimidating flurry of activity. Tables, too close together for comfort, are organized to hold sixteen and most tables seem to have a theme — kids who have interests in common sit together.

I couldn't locate Edward. I saw where the special education class was seated, accompanied by one of their aides. There were three students and a teacher's aide sitting at the end of one table near one of the three entryways into the lunchroom. At the far end of the table was another small group of students. The two groups didn't interact with one another. I asked the aide where Edward usually sat and she responded that he usually sits somewhere else, with his friends. She assured me he had plenty of friends in his lunch period.

I found Edward sitting alone at one end of a table made for sixteen.

Asperger's syndrome is a particularly challenging condition for kids who long to be connected to their peers. Edward is socially awkward enough that he has had a very difficult time engaging his peers.

Most high schoolers can only talk about *Halo*[1] for so long and are not terribly impressed by the complex storylines from Edward's home-made *Bionicle YouTube* videos. Furthermore, his excitement and enthusiasm about his chosen subject matter come across as aggression and quickly alienate his peers. As I sit down across from him, Edward opens, "This is a table for misfits — because I'm a misfit." He is, unfortunately, socially aware enough to be able to discern his own standing in the lunchroom. He directs my attention to the interactions around him and explains, in a voice that is inappropriately loud for the task, that he sits alone because he has no friends. Students around us cannot help but hear the conversation, but nobody argues. They know that if they did choose to sit with him they would be overwhelmed by his effort to connect with them (by talking incessantly about his own interests).

Edward has a strong desire to be connected with his peers. Sadly, the game is rigged against him. If he has to navigate the complex social world of high school relationships to win friends, he will always sit alone, he will always be an outsider, and he will remain on the margins, disconnected. His inability to read facial expressions and posture, his difficulty detecting peers' emotions or empathizing with them, combined with his limited range of age-appropriate interests translates into a devastating social deficit. I realized the moment I sat down with him that for Edward to have friends in high school, it would take an act of election by another student — a student who is spiritually mature enough to choose him outside of the usual social considerations.

I know Edward to be humorous, thoughtful, playful, and creative. I am not blind to the things that make his peers reject him; they simply don't matter to me.

Edward has a developmental disability. As Special Education scholar Erik Carter describes it, a developmental disability is "a label shared by an incredibly diverse group of people who often experience substantial difficulties in several major life activities — such as mobility, self-care, language, socialization, learning, or independent living. For these individuals," Carter continues, "their disabilities affect them cognitively and/or physically, and their need for support is expected to

---

1. I would describe *Halo* as a first-person shooter, science fiction, interstellar war video game. Edward would suggest that this description does the game a terrible injustice, but you get the idea.

last throughout their lifetimes."[2] Since nearly 20 percent of children are diagnosed with a developmental disability, that means: *if you are committed to youth ministry then you need to consider what it means to minister to and with adolescents with developmental disabilities.* A principled commitment to the idea of ministry with adolescents with developmental disabilities, "like-ing" the idea on your Facebook page, or believing in the value of it will not transform you or your congregation the way that participating in their lives as friends will. My purpose in writing this book is to consider the life experience of the nearly 20 percent of children under the age of eighteen who have a developmental disability, to draw out the profound consequences of this experience for ministry, and to promote an approach to ministry that accounts for their perspectives, faith responses, and witness.

This is a book about ministry and not about disability. Therefore, rather than dedicate space in this book to information about various disabilities (explaining etiologies, describing deficits, etc.) that can be found quite easily on the Internet, this book will promote a practice-centered model for ministry with adolescents and adolescents with developmental disabilities. I will attempt to support the following theses:

1. *One faithful and effective way to minister to and with adolescents and adolescents with developmental disabilities is to create spaces[3] through practice-centered ministry in which durable friendships can develop.*

2. Erik W. Carter, *Including People with Disabilities in Faith Communities: A Guide for Service Providers, Families, and Congregations* (Baltimore: Paul H. Brookes, 2007), p. 2.

3. My understanding of creating "space" is derived from Parker Palmer's discussion of education in *To Know as We Are Known: A Spirituality of Education* (San Francisco: Harper & Row, 1983). He explains that teaching is about creating space where the learning encounter can occur and in which "obedience to truth is practiced" (pp. 69-87). Palmer is addressing the fact that learning is impacted, either impeded or stimulated, by physical, emotional, psychological, and social spaces. My application from Palmer has been to recognize that Christian practices, as the curriculum of Christian formation, help to guide the *creation of spaces* in which students can be introduced to new ideas and can collaboratively investigate, evaluate, experience, and challenge the reality of God's faithful presence. Practices help to create space by guiding the organization of the physical arrangement and ethos of a room to make it more accessible and welcoming. Is the room a place where students are able to be fully present, where questions are welcomed, and students are heard, or is it a place where information is organized and disseminated with a rigid finality? Are there a variety of delivery systems that appeal to the broad range of learning styles and intelligences so students can demonstrate their competency in a variety of contexts? Space is created by biblical texts and the biblical narrative,

2. *When it comes to bearing witness to God's ongoing redemptive work in the world, nobody is impaired and they should not be disabled.*[4]

3. *Developing a proclamatory program* (our program includes all of our activities over the course of the year that support the ministry) *will help us to be more effective in reaching our friends with developmental disabilities and will increase our capacity to communicate the gospel more holistically.*

Key Concepts of the Book

When in seminary I asked a professor what book I should read to develop an understanding of Karl Barth's theology, she encouraged me to read Bruce McCormack's *Karl Barth's Critically Realistic Dialectical Theology: Its Genesis and Development 1909-1936.*[5] The title was almost enough to frighten me off. However, after consulting a theological dictionary (What is "realism" as opposed to "idealism"? What are "theological realism" and "critical realism"? What does he mean by "analogy" and "dialectic"?) and a Webster's Dictionary (I was not attuned to academic lingo at that time) and after reading the introduction, I had a pretty good idea of what was going to follow. In the paragraphs below I will expound the title of this book, *Amplifying Our Witness,* and its key concepts in hopes of providing some direction for what follows. The words were carefully chosen to tie together my academic training as a missiologist and my practical experience of ministering to and with adolescents with developmental disabilities.

---

which become a space that students and youth leaders can occupy together. Finally, space is created by mentors who recognize that people are more than a collection of instruments for cognition and who are hospitable to students who have developmental challenges or typically developing students who are experiencing the difficult "conversions" that attend the process of holistic learning.

4. The term "impairment" refers to a condition in and of itself: blindness, sensory-integration issues, a limited intellectual capacity, etc. The term "disability" relates to the relationship between the impaired individual and society. Disability is the result of an unaccommodating societal response to the impairment. For example, having difficulties walking due to cerebral palsy is impairment. Not being able to shower at a summer camp because you have nothing with which to support yourself in the shower is a disability.

5. Bruce L. McCormack, *Karl Barth's Critically Realistic Dialectical Theology: Its Genesis and Development 1909-1936* (Oxford: Clarendon Press, 2005).

Amplifying Our Witness

This book is about the witness of the church and how a plurality of voices and perspectives enhances our understanding of God and our community's witness to that God. The term "witness" (the Greek stem from which we get the word *martyr*) is 1. a person, 2. a testimony, and 3. a process of giving or bearing witness. The witnesses, their words and actions, point beyond themselves to the gracious action of God. Darrell Guder, who was a key figure in initiating the missional theology discussion, believes "witness" is a term that can comprehend the various aspects of a congregation's participation in the ongoing mission of God. As he explains, "[Witness/*marturia*] serves as an overarching term drawing together proclamation *(kerygma)*, community *(koinonia)*, and service *(diakonia)*. These are all essential dimensions of the Spirit-enabled witness for which the Christian church is called and sent."[6]

If bearing witness is what the church is "called and sent" to do, as Guder suggests, then we should find it particularly troubling that the witness of adolescents with developmental disabilities is rarely included in the testimony of the church. We place so much emphasis on human agency, competency in verbal communication, and individual initiative that we forget that we *bear* the witness of another, or as missionary scholar Lesslie Newbigin phrased it, "It is not that they must speak and act, asking the help of the Spirit to do so. It is rather that in their faithfulness to Jesus they become the place where the Spirit speaks and acts."[7]

While it is the Spirit who ultimately provides the power of the witness, we have a responsibility to participate in Christ's prophetic action to the extent our capacities allow us by being, doing, and saying the witness.[8] Adolescents with developmental disabilities have perspectives and experiences that can inform and contribute to the witness of the congregation. Too often, however, these gifts are marginalized or ignored. Our responsibility as partners with them is to amplify their witness in a number of ways, including offering them settings in which to use their gifts and making sure other people are aware of their con-

6. Darrell L. Guder, *The Continuing Conversion of the Church* (Grand Rapids: Eerdmans, 2000), p. 53.

7. Lesslie Newbigin, *The Gospel in a Pluralist Society* (Grand Rapids: Eerdmans, 1989), p. 118.

8. See Darrell L. Guder, *Be My Witnesses* (Grand Rapids: Eerdmans, 1985).

tributions to the community of faith. By employing the word "am-plify," I am insisting that people with disabilities have something to share that needs a hearing, something that our communities and churches can't do without.

Practice-Centered Ministry

The approach to ministry that I am advocating is practice-centered. This means that the curriculum for Christian discipleship is common participation in historic Christian practices like hospitality, forgiveness, prayer, friendship, honoring the body, etc. These practices are "Spirit-filled and embodied signs, instruments, and foretastes of the kingdom of God that Christian people participate in together over time to partake in, partner with, and witness to God's redemptive presence for the life of the world in Jesus Christ."[9]

In this book, I am arguing that by participating together with adolescents with developmental disabilities in Christian practices, especially the practice of friendship, we open up spaces where their faith and witness and ours will be nurtured and amplified.[10] While the past two decades have seen a proliferation of literature on Christian practices, Craig Dykstra is certainly a doyen of the practices discussion, and my understanding of Christian practices is deeply influenced by his theology of Christian practices.[11] Dykstra draws on Alasdair MacIntyre's conception of practices as explained in *After Virtue* and Edward

9. Benjamin T. Conner, *Practicing Witness: A Missional Vision of Christian Practices* (Grand Rapids: Eerdmans, 2011), p. 100.

10. Much of this introduction to Christian practices is excerpted from my article, Benjamin T. Conner, "Affirming Presence: Spiritual Life and Friendship with Adolescents with Developmental Disabilities," *International Journal of Children's Spirituality* 15, no. 4 (2010): 331-39.

11. Craig Dykstra, in his role as a practical theologian and as Lilly Endowment Senior Vice President, Religion, along with Dorothy Bass has supported the Practicing Our Faith conversation that has resulted in several books on the topic of Christian practices. The standard definition of practices according to this discourse is the following: "By 'Christian practices' we mean *things Christian people do together over time to address fundamental human needs in response to and in the light of God's active presence for the life of the world.*" Dykstra and Bass, "A Theological Understanding of Christian Practices," in *Practicing Theology: Beliefs and Practices in Christian Life,* ed. Miroslav Volf and Dorothy C. Bass (Grand Rapids: Eerdmans, 2001), p. 18, emphasis in original.

Farley's phenomenological theology.[12] Dykstra draws upon MacIntyre's theory of practices to make the distinction between a notion of practice, even strategic and patterned actions, carried out by professional agents to create change in other persons using social-scientific theories *outside of larger moral considerations* and his notion of Christian practices that is grounded in a community of faith. A mechanical view of practice may appear "effective" or "efficient" but misses the transformative element of *habitus,* the central motivating and organizing ideal of the community, and the state and disposition of the soul, or, as Dykstra puts it, "profound, life-orienting, identity-shaping participation in the constitutive practices of Christian life."[13]

There is another meaning of practice, argues Dykstra, which is a historically elongated, social, and communal way of responding to fundamental human conditions. For example, Christian friendship addresses, among other things, the fact that we are fundamentally communal beings, created to be in relationships. Any embodiment of the Christian tradition is contextual and participates in, modifies, and extends practices through which individuals and communities are able to realize goods that are internal to that tradition. In each new context, we learn more about what it means to be a friend. We learn more about the goods internal to friendship (intimacy, self-revelation, encounter of another) that are not available outside of such relationships. We recognize that there are also "goods" that are external to the practice of friendship (the relationship can be instrumental to any number of ends like achieving status, influence, or personal satisfaction).

To MacIntyre's insights, Dykstra adds Farley's appropriation of Edmund Husserl's studies in phenomenology that tie the apprehensions of the realities of faith to a community. Farley acknowledges a nonrational knowledge, a prereflective, preconscious perceptivity that is brought into existence as it is mediated through participation

---

12. MacIntyre's approach to practices is found in his *After Virtue: A Study in Moral Theology,* 2nd ed. (Notre Dame: University of Notre Dame Press, 1984). Farley's phenomenological theology is articulated in *Ecclesial Man: A Social Phenomenology of Faith and Reality* (Philadelphia: Fortress Press, 1975). Phenomenological theology is "the attempt to penetrate and describe the pre-reflective matrix of faith's acts and structures." Farley, *Ecclesial Man,* p. 51.

13. Craig R. Dykstra, "Reconceiving Practice," in *Shifting Boundaries: Contextual Approaches to the Structure of Theological Education,* ed. Barbara G. Wheeler and Edward Farley (Louisville: Westminster/John Knox Press, 1991), p. 50.

in the Christian community. Whether or not one completely agrees with Farley's argument, one can certainly agree that participation in a community of faith can have a transformative impact that may have more to do with intuition and impression than any cognitive appeal, and does not necessarily correspond to our intellectual or psychosocial development.[14]

Simply stated, practices like healing, hospitality, and Sabbath keeping are entrusted to us from our living historical traditions, and we shape them in the present to address our particular circumstances. Our practices persist in the present and are extended into the future because they find expression in social forms of embodiment. Our practices are universal in that they address fundamental human needs that are experienced across the globe, yet they are contextualized such that each practice is shaped to fit each culture. The practice of healing outside of the city in a sub-Saharan African country like Malawi, for example, while maintaining a family resemblance to the practice of healing in my home town of Williamsburg, Virginia, is textured and informed by the fact that it is practiced in a setting that includes a wider world of ancestral spirits, superstition, and witch doctors.[15] Whether in Malawi or Virginia, however, the practice of healing addresses the issues of illness, frailty, and finitude.[16] Finally, and most importantly for my argument, Christian practices have a transformational quality related to a spiritual reality such that participating in Christian practices puts one in a position to recognize, experience, and participate in God's active presence for the world.

In Dykstra's words, Christian practices are constitutive of "the

14. David Brooks has written an entertaining and well-researched book about the types of forces, beyond our intellect, that impact our development and decision making. As Brooks states in the introduction, "The research being done today reminds us of the relative importance of emotion over pure reason, social connections over individual choice, character over IQ, emergent, organic systems over linear, mechanistic ones, and the idea that we have multiple selves over the idea that we have a single self." David Brooks, *The Social Animal: The Hidden Sources of Love, Character, and Achievement* (New York: Random House, 2011), p. xiii.

15. See, for example, Janet Brown's work on HIV/AIDS in Malawi in her dissertation, "HIV/AIDS Alienation: Between Prejudice and Acceptance" (University of Stellenbosch, 2004).

16. See the excellent discussion of the practice of healing and care for the ill in Susan J. Dunlap, *Caring Cultures: How Congregations Respond to the Sick* (Waco, TX: Baylor University Press, 2009).

kind of community life through which God's presence is palpably felt and known" and "place us where we can receive a sense of the presence of God."[17] Participation in Christian practices opens the door for new ways of knowing through a kind of experiential knowledge that does not depend on one's cognitive capacities or developmental stage.

> [I]n the context of participation in certain practices we come to see more than just the value of the "good" of certain human activities. Beyond that, we may come to awareness of certain realities that outside of these practices are beyond our *ken*. Engagement in certain practices may give rise to new knowledge.[18]

From the standpoint of their capacity to create a space in which adolescent spirituality and faith are nurtured, Christian practices are *"habitations of the Spirit*, in the midst of which we are invited to participate in the practices of God."[19] For Dykstra, and in this regard I certainly follow Dykstra, the practices create spaces or arenas that put us in a position where we can be formed spiritually and, I would add, are particularly suited for the spiritual nurture of persons with developmental disabilities.

Finally, and importantly for this conversation, there is no intellectual capacity threshold necessary for participation in Christian practices. What intellectual capacities are required to be chosen as a friend, to be received as a guest, or to be a part of a community of prayer? Not only are Christian practices inclusive of all people, beyond that, by including the whole body of Christ in our practice of the faith, our friends with developmental disabilities challenge the adequacy and depth of our practice of the faith and subsequently, our theology. This is why I advocate practice-centered ministry as the way of discipleship for adolescents and adolescents with disabilities.

17. Craig R. Dykstra, *Growing in the Life of Faith: Education and Christian Practices,* 2nd ed. (Louisville: Westminster/John Knox Press, 2005), pp. 53 and 63, respectively.

18. Dykstra, "Reconceiving Practice," p. 145.

19. Dykstra, *Growing in the Life of Faith*, p. 78.

Adolescence

John Santrock, who wrote the book on adolescence, defines it as "the period of transition between childhood and adulthood that involves biological, cognitive, and socioemotional changes. A key task for adolescence is preparation for adulthood."[20] This means that adolescence begins in biology (the onset of puberty) and ends in sociology (assimilation into the adult world). The special place of adolescence has been the result of a unique set of social circumstances that have, as historian Joseph Kett and others have identified, resulted from "the emergence of a yawning time gap between the onset of sexual maturity and the full incorporation of young people into the economic life of the adult world."[21] Is a thirty-something living at home still an adolescent? Is a young man with a developmental disability perpetually an adolescent?

I understand adolescence in the United States to include a place, a path, and a purpose. Generally, as a result of a number of factors, the place of adolescence has been the high school where a youth culture has arisen. I realize that there are many disadvantaged kids who, for one reason or another, decide to or are required to stop attending high school. Nonetheless, an intense and protracted period of time with peers in school and in school-related activities, largely separated from adult influences, has led to the creation of a youth subculture. This subculture has, in turn, with the massive influence of an invested and savvy market that has discerned their disposable income and targeted them as consumers, determined what it means to be a teen.[22] For students with developmental disabilities, who are often segregated into separate classrooms if not separate schools, this place has been inhospitable. Even in its fragmentation and pluriformity of expressions, youth culture moves too quickly and connections within it remain elusive to persons with disabilities, making it difficult for them to participate in it or connect to it in any significant way.

Adolescence is a path because it begins in dependence under the care of a family and ends in full incorporation into the economic life of a society. This is a problem for the typically developing child because

20. John W. Santrock, *Adolescence,* 10th ed. (New York: McGraw-Hill, 2005), p. 21.

21. Joseph F. Kett, "Adolescence and Youth in Nineteenth-Century America," *Journal of Interdisciplinary History* 2, no. 2 (1971): 283.

22. See, for example, the PBS Frontline special, *Merchants of Cool,* available online at http://www.pbs.org/wgbh/pages/frontline/shows/cool/.

young people have been targeted as consumers and not encouraged to be producers. According to Côté and Allahar, "young people have been increasingly targeted as consumers of 'leisure industries' (e.g., media and music) and 'identity industries' (e.g., fashion and education)."[23] In fact, the very term "teenager" has its origin in advertising and marketing.[24] Identity becomes, under such conditions, externally grounded in something that is as stable and consistent as sand. If the path to incorporation in society is difficult for typically developing adolescents, where does that leave adolescents with developmental disabilities who have fewer opportunities to participate meaningfully in any aspect of our society? Another obvious issue is that the path of adolescence in America follows the values of our culture, which valorizes independence and seeks to avoid dependence. As John Swinton has stated, modern society judges the value of persons by the criteria of "independence, productivity, intellectual prowess and social position."[25] Many people with more profound disabilities will always be dependent and will never complete the path from childhood to a productive member of society that adolescence holds forth.

The purpose of adolescence is the task of discovering one's identity and preparation for adulthood and assumes progression through stages of development.[26] From a psychosocial standpoint, we expect a

23. James E. Côté and Anton L. Allahar, *Generation on Hold: Coming of Age in the Late Twentieth Century* (New York: New York University Press, 1994), p. xvi.

24. Thomas Hine, *The Rise and Fall of the American Teenager: A New History of the American Adolescent Experience* (New York: HarperCollins, 2000), p. 8.

25. John Swinton, "The Body of Christ Has Down's Syndrome: Theological Reflections on Vulnerability, Disability, and Graceful Communities," *Journal of Pastoral Theology* 13, no. 2 (Fall 2003): 67.

26. I am not unaware of recent challenges to stage theories of development. For example, proponents of dynamic systems theory suggest that typical developmental theories are unable to account for the interaction between various factors that impact development. As Howe and Lewis explain, "the child is an emergent self-organizing system, continuously changing or stabilizing in interaction with an environment, rather than a trajectory programmed by genetics, normative stages, or any other static variable." Mark L. Howe and Marc D. Lewis, "The Importance of Dynamic Systems Approaches for Understanding Development," *Developmental Review* 25 (2005): 251. In fact, Marc Lewis makes the claim that systems theory can help account for "the creation of order from intrinsic process, the increase in complexity over time, the emergence of true novelty within developing systems, transition points that permit both structural advances and individual diversification, and the capacity for self-correcting stability as well as sensitive adaptation to the environment." Marc D. Lewis, "The Promise of Dy-

typically developing adolescent to crave both independence and guidance, to try on new identities as they understand themselves through the eyes of others, to be on the lookout for something worthy to give themselves to, to define themselves in terms of a group, and be loyal to a fault. As they develop cognitively, they begin to be able to hypothesize and test possibilities in their mind. They can think about thought and become interested in clarifying their beliefs. They are idealists.

The development of these psychosocial and cognitive competencies has consequences for how they express their faith, according to James Fowler.[27] Adolescents might imagine God as a "best friend" and use others to provide mirrors for their own beliefs. They are looking for a "faith worth dying for" and are highly critical of hypocrisy. All of these changes occur in complex systems and are accompanied by growth spurts, sexual maturation, and hormones, hormones, hormones in such a way that makes Erikson's description of it seem simplistic: "Adolescence is the last stage of childhood. The adolescent process, however, is conclusively complete only when the individual has subordinated his childhood identifications to a new kind of identification, achieved in absorbing sociability and in competitive apprenticeship with and among his age mates."[28]

The obvious issue for people who minister among adolescents with developmental disabilities is, the kids we work with don't develop in this expected pattern. If we limit our understanding of one's spiritu-

---

namic Systems Approaches for an Integrated Account of Human Development," *Child Development* 71, no. 1 (February 2000): 39. Glenn Cupit draws upon systems theory to consider the nature of spiritual development and to challenge reigning stage theories, concluding, "Current approaches to human development are not conducive to consideration of matters of spirituality, because of their adherence to a linear paradigm incompatible with most conceptualizations of the nature of the spirit." C. Glenn Cupit, "The Marriage of Science and Spirit: Dynamic Systems Theory and the Development of Spirituality," *International Journal of Children's Spirituality* 12, no. 2 (August 2007): 114-15. In all theories of development, systems or stage, there is still the notion of someone moving from point A to point B, and when we take the spirituality of people with developmental disabilities seriously we find no theory accounts for the mysterious movement of God. In this book I am addressing, primarily, approaches to spiritual nurture that have been founded on stage theories of development simply because these theories have been the dominant approaches.

27. James Fowler, *Stages of Faith: The Psychology of Human Development and the Quest for Meaning* (San Francisco: Harper & Row, 1981).

28. Erik Erikson, *Identity, Youth and Crisis* (New York: W. W. Norton, 1968), p. 155.

ality in terms of age-appropriate moral growth or verbal affirmations of
faith that accompany cognitive developments, then we will likely miss
what kids with developmental disabilities have to offer. The assumption
is that along with the spiritual encounter, adolescents will develop in
their moral convictions with the complexity, intentionality, and responsibility that are appropriate to other persons their age. But it must be
considered that spiritual growth is not strictly tied to human development. It is also true that at different times, related to different intellectual and emotional capacities, the process of spiritual growth will take
on different manifestations, as Kenda Dean has made clear in her work
on the faith responses of adolescents.[29] For example, adolescence opens
up new possibilities for spiritual formation with the introduction of
formal operational thinking, the ability to consider abstract possibilities, and the surge of passion that leaves them looking for something
worth dying for. All of these new resources are activated in the spiritual
encounter. But what happens to those who don't develop along the predictable course and don't seem to have these capacities?

Karen Marie Yust's observations about faith in children could be
aptly applied to spirituality among adolescents with developmental
disabilities. Consider the implications of this statement for understanding the spirituality of adolescents with disabilities:

> My call for defining faith as a gift from God rather than a set of be-
> liefs or a well-developed cognitive understanding of all things spiri-
> tual is, then, an attempt to encourage us to take seriously this ten-
> sion from the "grace" side of the equation so that children are
> recognized as fully [spiritual] beings from birth. If we hold this def-
> inition of faith as an act of grace, then we make room for children
> to be actual people of faith rather than just potential people of
> faith in need of further development before they can truly engage
> in a spiritual life. If faith is not something we do but something we
> are given by God, then anyone can be a recipient of faith and re-
> spond with faithfulness, even if that person is incapable of rational
> reasoning.[30]

29. Kenda C. Dean, *Practicing Passion: Youth and the Quest for a Passionate Church*
(Grand Rapids: Eerdmans, 2004).

30. Karen Marie Yust, *Real Kids, Real Faith: Practices for Nurturing Children's Spiritual
Lives* (San Francisco: Jossey-Bass, 2004), p. 7.

At each age and stage of development children have certain abilities and primary activities. While developmental theory seems to push us forward to the next, emerging stage of spiritual development, Christian educators who are interested in spiritual formation must be attuned to the capabilities that emerge in each stage through which kids can embody their faith. But what if those capacities never emerge? Webb-Mitchell draws upon an unpublished manuscript by Robert Schalock, one-time president of the AAMR (American Association of Mental Retardation), to challenge, "Among professionals in the health care field, some are even suggesting that spiritual awareness, or more precisely an awareness of God, is only marginally related to intelligence, if at all."[31]

A program of spiritual nurture that relies on the cognitive exercises of memorizing and repeating doctrine seems insufficient to the task. In the historic practice of Christian catechism, catechesis means to teach by word of mouth or, more literally, to "echo back." In order for Christian catechism to be inclusive, kids with developmental disabilities need to be afforded a space in which they can "echo back" according to their own capacities and abilities and in their own manner. We cannot limit our expectations and impressions of the spiritual vitality of adolescents with developmental disabilities simply because they don't proceed through the expected stages of human development. Instead, through participating together in Christian practices we allow a certain freedom for spiritual encounter and create an atmosphere or environment in which the adolescent with special needs can interiorize the symbols, respond to spiritual realities, and experience community in their own way, according to their own abilities and disabilities, like everyone else.

My Biased Perspective *(as Opposed to Your Biased Perspective)*

I can't escape the fact, nor would I want to, that I am a practitioner of ministry with adolescents with developmental disabilities who has been academically trained as a missiologist. My theological education has occurred in seminaries that adhere to the Reformed tradition, broadly understood, and in the prosaic activities and exigencies of life spent with

31. Brett Webb-Mitchell, *God Plays Piano, Too: The Spiritual Lives of Disabled Children* (New York: Crossroad, 1993), p. 94.

people who are often neglected, underappreciated, or misunderstood. Consequently, my practice and theology of ministry are being constantly challenged and reformed by my experience of ministry and the often-surprising encounter with the ongoing redemptive work of God in the midst of pedestrian activities. The two most significant lenses that I apply to my theological inquiry and my community's practice of ministry are those of practical theology and missional theology.

Practical Theology

Two scholars who have influenced my understanding of practical theology are John Swinton and Rick Osmer. John Swinton, a practical theologian at Aberdeen, leader in the field of disability studies, and one whose theology of friendship we will visit in later chapters, offers a concise and mission-informed definition of practical theology.

> A basic definition would be that practical theology is theological reflection on the praxis of the church as it strives to remain faithful to the continuing mission of the Triune God in, to, and for the world. Practical theology seeks to guide and critique ecclesial praxis as the church strives to fulfill its role as "the hermeneutic of the gospel," which is the place where the gospel is lived out and interpreted to the world through the actions and character of its participants.[32]

To expound this definition, it should be noted that practical theology is not "applied" theology, as if theology is done somewhere else (academy) and then applied by a professional (clergy) to a specific context (congregation). Practical theology is critical reflection on the action of the church in the world. To this process Swinton adds a sense of purpose. The actions of the church are evaluated in the light of the calling of the church to participate in the "continuing mission of God in, to, and for the world." The church is, Swinton states, following Newbigin, the "hermeneutic of the gospel."[33]

Swinton's missional approach to practical theology is encapsulated in his statement that the church is the "hermeneutic of the gos-

---

32. Swinton, "The Body of Christ Has Down's Syndrome," pp. 66-67.
33. Newbigin, *The Gospel in a Pluralist Society,* pp. 222-33.

pel." This concept carries two primary meanings. First, the church becomes the authentication of the gospel to the surrounding culture to the degree that its life and message are congruent with the life of the kingdom of God (lived out and interpreted to the world through the character and actions of the congregation). Second, the church with its plausibility structures offers not only the external example of life in accordance with the gospel but also a vantage point and the lenses through which one can properly understand the gospel.

To this definition I add Richard Osmer's process of practical theological reflection. Osmer, Professor of Christian Education at Princeton Theological Seminary, argues that practical theological reflection is a process that helps us discern the faithfulness of our practice of faith in concrete situations. The process begins with the question, "What is going on?" — a question that requires familiarizing oneself with the patterns and dynamics of certain practices by carefully attending to the people and events being considered. Next, theories of the arts and sciences (usually social science) are employed to answer the question, "Why is this going on in this way?" In response to this question, the theological assumptions that guide a community's practices will be uncovered. Next, practical theologians draw upon theological resources to interpret Christian practices in order to construct "theological and ethical norms by which to critically assess, guide, and reform some dimension of contemporary religious praxis."[34] The normative question being asked in coordination with the establishment of theological norms is, "What ought to be going on?" Finally, the pragmatic question is addressed: "How might we respond?" or "How might this area of praxis be shaped to embody more fully the normative commitments of a religious tradition in this particular context of experience?"[35] The pragmatic task of practical theology is executed by servant leaders who are capable of both determining influential strategies of action and leading a congregation in change.[36]

34. Richard R. Osmer and Friedrich L. Schweitzer, eds., *Developing a Public Faith: New Directions in Practical Theology* (St. Louis: Chalice Press, 2003), p. 3.

35. Osmer and Schweitzer, eds., *Developing a Public Faith,* p. 4.

36. Osmer's approach is similar to Groome's five-step approach of naming present action, critically reflecting on it, making accessible the Christian story and vision (the normative criteria), placing the story in dialectical conversation with the present practice, and finally focusing decisions or responses made for living the Christian life which are to be lived (a potential sixth movement). From Thomas H. Groome, *Sharing*

I have generally followed this pattern in my work with adolescents with developmental disabilities. I have found that the simple presence of such friends in my life has raised important foundational theological questions as well as pragmatic questions with respect to the practice of faith. Is my understanding of faith broad enough to include my friends with developmental disabilities? Do I cast a vision for Christian discipleship that requires competencies my friends don't have? Is my understanding of the image of God skewed by an intellectual bias? I have had to return to my theological resources in an effort to respond faithfully to these questions.

Missional Theology

This book is an exercise in a particular type of practical theology called missional theology. As I have written elsewhere, "Missional theology is a kind of practical theology that explores in every aspect of the theological curriculum and praxis of the church the implications of the missionary nature of God with the purpose of forming congregations to better articulate the gospel and to live faithfully their vocation to participate in the ongoing redemptive mission of God in a particular context."[37]

Directly above I have explained my understanding of practical theology, so when I indicate that missional theology is a kind of practical theology, I am suggesting that it is disciplined theological reflection that is concerned with congregational practices and their faithfulness to the mission of God. What makes it "missional"? The overarching conviction that God's mission must be the starting point for the theological enterprise, and that it must inform and orient the way the Christian faith is practiced. Missional theology orients practical theology such that "All of our theological resources must be marshaled for the formation of the church, in each particular community, for empowered proclamation of the gospel in its midst and faithful witness in the world."[38]

Faith: A Comprehensive Approach to Religious Education and Pastoral Ministry: The Way of Shared Praxis (San Francisco: Harper, 1991), pp. 146-48.

37. Conner, *Practicing Witness,* p. 11.

38. Darrell L. Guder, "Missional Theology for a Missional Church," *Journal for Preachers* 22, no. 1 (1988): 9.

The term "missional" calls the church to remember that the church is chosen for something, a vocation beyond itself; church life is eccentric. God's sending action, the election of the missionary God, constitutes the church and gives it purpose — to participate in the witness of God.

Missional theology is contextual theology in that it espouses a methodology that considers the relationship between a local congregation, the gospel, and its cultural setting. Since missional theology addresses a universal concern (the gospel) in a way that is local and contextual, it emphasizes the cultural pluriformity of the gospel. As Newbigin has explained: ". . . as the mission goes its way to the ends of the earth new treasures are brought into the life of the Church and Christianity itself grows and changes until it becomes more credible as a foretaste of the unity of all humankind."[39] Newbigin's insights apply equally to the impact that including adolescents with developmental disabilities in our congregational life can have on our doctrine and witness.

Structure of the Book

Chapter two will dig deeper into Edward's sense of being disconnected by describing the issues that are a part of the daily experience of adolescents with developmental disabilities. It will also address some of the obstacles that confront young persons with disabilities who desire a sense of connectedness — like being dissed, labeled, lonely, and often without peer or congregational support. In the third chapter, I will share the experiences and theological processes that have led me to a way of ministry I think of as "affirming presence." A brief exploration of the theological concept of *imago Dei*, or the image of God, will lead into a discussion about Christian friendship as the central practice of a ministry of affirming presence. I will make the case that relationships should be considered sacramental and not instrumental, highlight the importance of the doctrine of election in establishing friendships, and address honestly the inconvenience of friendship. In the fourth chapter the theological concept of *missio Dei*, or the mission of God, will guide a discussion about the iconic and evocative witness of adolescents with developmental disabilities. I will advocate "amplifying our witness" as

39. Newbigin, *The Gospel in a Pluralist Society*, pp. 123-24.

one way we can demonstrate mutuality in ministry, and I will cast a vision for friendship as a missional Christian practice. In the fifth chapter, after introducing the concept of *opus Dei,* or the work of God, I will articulate my practical theology for ministry with adolescents and adolescents with developmental disabilities. This is not a template to be applied without modification to another context, but it does demonstrate one way that one ministry to adolescents with developmental disabilities has attempted to be faithful. I will argue that a proclamatory program of practicing faith together set within the context of hospitable settings and relationships creates spaces where we can encounter one another and God at work among us. In an epilogue I will consider how a life shared with adolescents with developmental disabilities can inform our theology of evangelism.

Through this book I intend to stimulate an ongoing discussion about the contribution of adolescents with developmental disabilities to our theology and practice of ministry. When you have finished reading it you might feel as if I have pushed you in a particular direction. Feel free to push back.

chapter 2

Awakened to the Issues

Visio Dei

> *"All he does after school is play his Xbox."*
> *"What about friends?"*
> *"He used to hang out with a boy down the street. Then one of that boy's friends asked him, 'Why do you hang out with a retard?' Now, well, he doesn't really have any."*

Awakened to the Issues

On Christmas morning my son opened his longboard, a 48″ skateboard variant made for downhill adventures. Half an hour later he was being loaded onto an ambulance after a devastating crash. Three days later he was in intensive care insisting to the nurse that my name was "Pache." I did not know then that everything was going to be fine. I did know that if he were to have a diminished intellectual capacity as a result of his accident, it would not affect my fatherly love for him or my brotherly friendship with him. It was my time being with kids with developmental disabilities that made the experience with my son less frightening. I was awakened to the issues facing adolescents with developmental disabilities and their parents four years ago. Now I sometimes forget that people whom others consider disabled surround me.

In Catholic theology the *visio Dei* is the beatific vision, the perception of God. German mystic Meister Eckhart, however, suggested that we not seek the *visio Dei* in heaven alone, but instead, "see things in this life as God sees them."[1] It is in this sense that I am using *visio Dei*.

Emmanuel's Gift

I was trying to make a point about how kids with developmental disabilities can make important contributions to their school, community, and church by using the film *Emmanuel's Gift*, a story about a Ghanaian with a stigmatizing physical disability who overcame adversity to become an advocate for people with physical disabilities in his country and around the world. This was at a meeting we call *Student Leader Training*, a regularly scheduled meeting in our ministry that is open to typically developing, mainstream high school kids and kids with developmental disabilities. Most of the kids who attend have some sort of impairment. I was trying to stress the point that, according to the film, 10 percent of Ghanaians have some sort of disability, so I said significantly, "Look around the room. That would mean that out of our group two or three of you would have a disability!" The other leaders stared at me, befuddled by my observation. It simply had not occurred to me at that moment that most of the people in the room had some sort of disability.

According to the National Center on Birth Defects and Developmental Disability, around 17 percent of children younger than eighteen have a developmental disability[2] and one in every 110 children is diagnosed with some form of autism.[3] In other words, kids with developmental disabilities are going to be a part of our future. If you are committed to youth ministry, then you will need to start learning about how to minister with adolescents with developmental disabilities.

Dissed

Why should Edward sit alone in a room full of peers? There is no arguing against the fact that people with autism have impairments and so-

1. Daniel G. Groody, "Crossing the Divide: Foundations of a Theology of Migration and Refugees," *Theological Studies* 70 (2009): 660.
2. National Center on Birth Defects and Developmental Disability website, http://www.cdc.gov/ncbddd/AboutUs/index.html, accessed February 6, 2011.
3. Autism Speaks website, http://www.autismspeaks.org/whatisit/index.php, accessed February 6, 2011.

cial deficits; however, it is our culture that disables. From a medical and sociocultural standpoint, Autism Spectrum Disorder (ASD) is marked by qualitative impairments in social interaction and communication, restricted interests, difficulty in perceiving social cues, especially non-verbal social cues, lack of social or emotional reciprocity, and theory-of-mind issues (mind blindness — they are often unaware that others perceive the world differently from themselves, are not sensitive to the feelings, perceptions, perspectives, desires, and knowledge of others). People on the autism spectrum aren't typically able to initiate or sustain conversations, have a tendency toward concrete thinking, generally lack the ability to engage in imaginative age-appropriate play, often have inflexible routines, tend to engage in repetitive motor movements, can be hypersensitive to sounds, smells, taste, or light. They often have difficulty in establishing affective connections with others and can't traverse the landscape of interactions or discern the nuances of emotional relationships effectively. Does any of this make people with ASD unworthy of being chosen as friends or included in a community or loved?

Think about someone being "dis"enfranchised. Disenfranchisement occurs when some entity or group of people is depriving another person or group of a benefit of citizenship — for example, the right to vote or to have their vote counted. The problem is not with the one attempting to exercise citizenship — the problem is with the system that denies that person or group access to the means of exercising citizenship. In a similar way, when one is dis-abled, the problem is not really that they have impairments and social skill deficits. The issue at stake is that they live in an "ableist" culture that rarely affords them the space or opportunity to make their unique contribution to society and does not lift up the value of choosing them as friends. Those with developmental impairments have been, as a result of their differences, dis-abled or dissed. The sad truth about our culture is well articulated by ethicist Hans Reinders: "What ultimately prevents people with intellectual disabilities from full participation in our society is the fact that they are generally not seen as people we want to be present in our lives. We don't need them. . . . They are rarely chosen as friends."[4] We simply are not willing to readjust our lives to make room for them.[5]

4. Hans S. Reinders, *Receiving the Gift of Friendship: Profound Disability, Theological Anthropology, and Ethics* (Grand Rapids: Eerdmans, 2008), p. 142.

5. "The will to give ourselves to others and 'welcome' them, to readjust our identi-

Society makes it incredibly difficult for people with social skill deficits, cognitive impairment, or other limitations to be included because they fail to fit into the dominant narrative of the good life. As John Swinton explains, "People with learning disabilities are not only disadvantaged because of their condition, they are also disadvantaged by the way they are perceived by society, and the effect that their presence has upon the hopes and expectations that underpin that society."[6] It is our inability to handle strangeness and difference that leads us to allow impairments to become disabling. Accordingly, Amos Yong has argued that disabilities are "as much if not more, social, cultural, economic, and political constructions as they are biological, cognitive, and genetic conditions."[7] Adolescents with developmental disabilities are strangers.

Strangers are people without a place, detached from basic life-supporting institutions like family, work, religious community, or the networks of relations that sustain us. In our economically driven, results-oriented society, many kids and adults with developmental disabilities are irrelevant because they live outside of the economic system. Furthermore, they are simply too different to fit into the reigning narrative of what comprises the "good life."

I am not denying that my friends with developmental disabilities have differences that make a difference. Their impairments make a difference in how they might gather or process information and, consequently, how they interact with others. But differences need not be dehumanizing or a source of isolation. I am simply suggesting that impairment is a difference that should not make a difference when it comes to being befriended, loved, and cherished.

Special Olympics, the Arc, and other organizations have provided opportunities for the humanization of those with special needs. For example, my daughter has swimming goals that include being the fastest freestyler in her age group in the state of Virginia. My son has a swimming goal of simply qualifying for a local championship meet. My

ties to make space for them, is prior to any judgment about others, except that of identifying them in their humanity." In Miroslav Volf, *Exclusion and Embrace: A Theological Exploration of Identity, Otherness, and Reconciliation* (Nashville: Abingdon, 1996), p. 29.

6. John Swinton and Esther McIntosh, "Persons in Relation: The Care of Persons with Learning Disabilities," *Theology Today* 57, no. 2 (2000): 180-81.

7. Amos Yong, *Theology and Down Syndrome: Reimagining Disability in Late Modernity* (Waco, TX: Baylor University Press, 2007), pp. 80-81.

friend John has equally ambitious and competitive swimming goals through Special Olympics that are commensurate with his abilities. All three competitors have embraced legitimate and challenging goals that include authentic ways of entering into athletic competition and the practice of swimming. And all three competitors are swimmers, just like Michael Phelps, even if they look limited and incompetent when compared to him. One of my friends, a brilliant pastor and author who also happens to be a self-described "bed-ridden quadriplegic," has stated that *everyone* is limited — for elite athletes we call these limits world records.

Labels

What do you do when you are at a camp designed for kids with disabilities and one of your campers, who happens to have Asperger's syndrome, is in the middle of a crowd of peers with Down syndrome yelling at them and calling them "retards" because he feels excluded from their game? He is socially aware enough to detect a difference between himself and the others, and, consequently, has feelings of loneliness and exclusion, but he is unable to empathize with them as one who has himself been labeled and ridiculed. He does not realize that by employing a hurtful label to others he is perpetuating a culture that will destroy him.[8]

One thing I hear people say about labels, in defense of using them, is "But it's *true*." In other words, the person *is* obese, the person *is* Oriental, the person *is* retarded. What they miss is that it actually *isn't* true, in that the way the label is used represents or creates a distortion of reality. When we label others, we potentially limit the scope of our relationship by focusing attention on a certain way of knowing them. Labels often emphasize caricatures and focus on deficits and limitations, and in this way there are things they obscure or don't tell us. People with autism or with Down syndrome are not a homogeneous group — they are individuals. Even in our typical relationships, for example, we would never proclaim, "Bryce is my white, middle-class, straight, able-bodied, protestant friend." He is just Bryce in all of his Bryce-ness,

---

8. This also turned out to be an excellent opportunity to talk about the issue of sin.

and the labels do as much to limit one's understanding of Bryce as they do to explain him. Since labels are political and social constructions, they generate "asymmetric relationships."[9] To say "Gibson has MR and cerebral palsy" is to ensure that he will not have a chance to make a fresh first impression and to orient others toward his impairments rather than his possibilities, relationships, and gifts. This is why we use "people-first" language in the field of disability studies.

Another danger with labeling is that it perpetuates stereotypes and misconceptions. Most people who don't have friends or family members with Down syndrome haven't witnessed the personhood of such individuals. They are among "the disabled," a generic, nameless group of persons with whom we don't desire to and can't imagine how to connect in any deep and meaningful way. When this is the case, when we dehumanize a person into the category of "the disabled" it becomes easier to deny their experience of being human and to project how we imagine we would feel onto the person with disabilities. We might conclude, "If I were like that I'd rather be dead" or "I wouldn't want to live life like that." We might even be moved to social action and advocacy as a result of our sense of their condition. Of course, one problem with this way of thinking is that it appeals to our basest enlightened self-interest and our efforts don't account for the reality of the other.[10] It also fails to recognize that we can't see things from another's perspective. Most kids I know who have developmental disabilities, apart from loneliness (something that would make anyone's life miserable), are quite joyful and happy.

American journalist and political commentator George Will candidly wonders why so many medical professionals consider joyful people like his son, who has Down syndrome, unworthy of life. He concludes, "Jon experiences life's three elemental enjoyments — loving, being loved and ESPN. For Jon, as for most normal American males, the rest of life is details." There simply is not a lot required of us, from either an intellectual or psychosocial standpoint, to be loved. Unfortunately, in the case of Down syndrome, the label can be a death sentence. As Will explains, the American Congress of Obstetricians and Gynecologists' (ACOG) ostensibly value-neutral guidelines on informing parents with children who potentially have Down syndrome of the options

---

9. Groody, "Crossing the Divide," p. 643.
10. Reinders, *Receiving the Gift of Friendship,* pp. 140-41.

available to them are far from neutral. Will explains, "But what is antiseptically called 'screening' for Down syndrome is, much more often than not, a search-and-destroy mission: At least 85 percent of pregnancies in which Down syndrome is diagnosed are ended by abortions."[11]

James Overboe, a sociologist who has cerebral palsy, recognizes this desire to label another's life as issuing from a type of "genetic fundamentalism." Overboe argues that "genetic fundamentalism" negates "expressions of life" deemed disabled. By idealizing a vision of prototypical human embodiment and reducing people to biological essences via courtroom decisions and prenatal testing, genetic fundamentalism advances a vision of what sort of life is worth being lived and determines what genes can contribute to such a life. In agreement with Will, Overboe argues that genetic screening suggests the invalidity of some expressions of humanity: "The forecasting of a bleak future for disabled people placed outside normality legitimizes the eradication of prospective disabled people."[12]

Is living with a disability an unacceptable way of being human? It is worth considering whether retardation or autism would even "exist" in a society that valued cooperation over competition, interdependence over independence. Are we under the false belief that we can eliminate all impairments? The fact that there are environmental or accidental causes of impairment that occur after birth suggests that it is impossible to eliminate people with impairments. What of suffering, or of the naturally disabling and socially acceptable condition of ageing? Is our lack of imagination impairing our ability to relate to nearly 20 percent of the adolescents to whom we are called to minister?[13]

11. George F. Will, "Will: The Attack on Kids with Down Syndrome," *Newsweek* (January 29, 2007). Archived from the original on May 17, 2007. Available at http://web.archive.org/web/20070516125514/http://www.msnbc.msn.com/id/16720750/site/newsweek. Amy Julia Becker, who has a daughter with Down syndrome, has written a book on the issue, and writes the blog *Thin Places,* helped to clarify the issue for me in the following correspondence: "While I certainly agree with your overall point, it's a little more complicated than this paragraph suggests. ACOG now recommends screening for all women, regardless of age, but only 2% of women choose amnios after the screening. Of those 2% a certain number find out the baby has Downs, and then 85% abort. In other words, it is a somewhat self-selecting group" (correspondence April 15, 2011).

12. James Overboe, "Disability and Genetics: Affirming the Bare Life (the State of Exception)," *Canadian Review of Sociology and Anthropology* 44, no. 2 (2007): 223.

13. "Unable to see like the retarded, to hear like the retarded, we attribute to them our suffering. We thus rob them of the opportunity to do what each of us must do —

One of the things I fear about this book is that someone might read it in hopes of learning what they can do for adolescents with developmental disabilities. That is not my purpose at all. The challenge of this book is that we need to learn to be for adolescents with disabilities by being with them. If we desire to minister with adolescents with developmental disabilities, then our relationship with them is not a client–service provider relationship or one based on pathology in which we try to cure them. If we desire mutuality in our ministry with adolescents with special needs, then our relationship with them needs to be one of Christian friendship. When we offer ourselves as friends we are already doing something with kingdom-of-God significance — we are giving them a new label, "friend," and are, thereby, de-stigmatizing them. As Webb-Mitchell states, "people with disabling conditions are not just another social action project for our churches. This is not social posturing; this is kingdom-of-God ethics ruling."[14] We are saying that they are not objects that receive charity, service, or cure; they are friends with whom we share life. We don't focus on the disabling condition (and we don't deny it, either), but we do all we can to transform the disabling culture that is the real reason they have not been able to find full inclusion in our churches and communities.

"Aching Emptiness"

"In Lake Wobegon even the atheists are Lutheran because it is the Lutheran God they don't believe in."

Garrison Keillor

I don't usually call upon Garrison Keillor as a theological resource, but in this instance, he is correct. Atheism is parasitic, so when people make the faith choice not to believe in God they certainly have some conception of God in mind that they are rejecting. For many persons with physical and developmental disabilities it is the combination of

learn to bear and live with our individual sufferings." Stanley Hauerwas, "Suffering the Retarded: Should We Prevent Retardation?" in *Critical Reflections on Stanley Hauerwas' Theology of Disability: Disabling Society, Enabling Theology*, ed. John Swinton (Binghamton, NY: Haworth Pastoral Press, 2004), p. 101.

14. Brett Webb-Mitchell, *God Plays Piano, Too: The Spiritual Lives of Disabled Children* (New York: Crossroad, 1993), p. 48.

an "ableist" conception of God (which is almost like Ludwig Feuerbach's vision of God as our best capacities magnified and projected) and the lack of close personal relationships to incarnate the love of that God that makes God seem distant and un-believable. Adolescents with developmental disabilities are often disconnected from their peers, from congregations, and from other sources of meaning and identity. Consequently many adolescents with developmental disabilities are lonely, spending a majority of their time at home alone in front of a television, a computer, or a video game system.

Richard Amado draws upon Perlman and Peplau's definition of loneliness as "the unpleasant experience that occurs when a person's network of social relationships is significantly deficient in either quality or quantity," and presents loneliness as "aching emptiness."[15] He explains, "The 'aching emptiness' of loneliness is a physiological phenomenon, a biological reaction to certain external events. Weiss suggests this physiological reaction is provoked by an absence of individual and community relationships." He continues to explain the psychosomatic consequences of loneliness (headaches, reduced appetite, tiredness), the connection between heart-related illness and loneliness, and the fact that people who are socially isolated face a higher mortality risk than those who smoke![16]

Several researchers have emphasized that not only do children with disabilities engage in fewer social, recreational, and leisure activities, but when they do participate in such activities they do so primarily with parents or other adults. What they are missing is the peer-to-peer relationships, and therefore the friendship development that typically developing children experience.[17] The situation is even more severe for minorities.[18]

15. Richard S. Amado, "Loneliness: Effects and Implications," in *Friendships and Community Connections between People with and without Developmental Disabilities,* ed. Angela Novak Amado (Baltimore: Paul H. Brookes, 1993), p. 68.

16. Amado, "Loneliness: Effects and Implications," pp. 70-71.

17. Abbie Solish, Adrienne Perry, and Patricia Minnes, "Participation of Children with and without Disabilities in Social, Recreational and Leisure Activities," *Journal of Applied Research in Intellectual Disabilities* 23, no. 3 (May 2010): 226-36.

18. In the late 1960s and early 1970s, labeling African American children as "mildly mentally retarded" was a way to bypass *Brown v. Board of Education* and continue to segregate black children. Even today a disproportionate representation of African American and other students of color has persisted in special education classes. On the other hand, argues Blanchett, the label of learning disabled (LD) has been historically reserved

If our encounters with people with disabilities are infrequent and episodic, we might never reflect on the importance of embodiment in friendship or the barriers faced by persons with disabilities that accompany impairment and often contribute to feelings of emptiness, loneliness, and isolation. There are barriers of transportation and locomotion; there are financial barriers; there is the issue of control (they don't get a driver's license and the accompanying ticket to freedom). As O'Brien and O'Brien explain, "People with developmental disabilities are often socially disembodied. Friendships emerge among a variety of social relationships, including being part of a family, having a life partner, being a neighbor, being part of a workplace, and being a member of community associations."[19] A life without such connections is a lonely and negated life. Mary McClintock Fulkerson envisions the church as "a place to appear," and as such, attempts to challenge the church's complicity in disembodying people with disabilities, often in the form of "obliviousness" or a "kind of experiential and geographical disregard that forms an a priori social condition of widely acknowledged injustice."[20] She considers Christian practices to be embodied theology that allows one to consider the fundamental beliefs of a congregation in terms of its members' ordinary life activities as well as liturgical practices. Alterations in the worship service can make the church a more hospitable place and can change the culture of the church. People with disabilities must be present in our congregations:

> Being seen and heard by others, being acknowledged by others of
> different social locations — this is essential to political life. It is also

for privileged white male students while their black or brown counterparts have received other, more stigmatizing labels (emotional and behavioral disorders or mildly mentally retarded). The practical consequence is that "middle and upper class white students with LD receive accommodations and modifications within the general education classroom setting while students of color with the same labels are educated in a self-contained setting." Wanda J. Blanchett, "Telling It Like It Is: The Role of Race, Class, and Culture in the Perpetuation of Learning Disability as a Privileged Category for the White Middle Class," *Disability Studies Quarterly* 30, no. 2 (2010). Online at http://www.dsq-sds.org/article/view/1233, accessed December 31, 2010.

19. John O'Brien and Connie Lyle O'Brien, "Unlikely Alliances: Friendships and People with Developmental Disabilities," in Amado, ed., *Friendships and Community Connections between People with and without Developmental Disabilities,* p. 24.

20. Mary McClintock Fulkerson, "A Place to Appear: Ecclesiology as if Bodies Mattered," *Theology Today* 64 (2007): 159.

essential to a community of faith. Of course, unless our habituations into the proprieties of dominant groups are transgressed in some way by "others," our well-meaning obliviousness and its accompanying unintended consequences will continue.[21]

Franklin has ASD, and it is possible to discern his engagement and excitement by his bouncing — strong, excited leaps he takes across the room. In simple terms, Fulkerson is saying that Franklin needs a place to bounce, and congregations need bouncing Franklins to open them up to different ways of being. If Franklin has no place to appear, then his contribution to the body will be negated.

Practical theologian James Loder addresses the concept of negation in terms of loneliness, rejection, embarrassment, and disorientation or a sense of meaninglessness that stretches through our lives. Loder sees in the trauma of birth the psychoanalytical roots of our fundamental human need to be connected. All of the newborn's activities are an attempt to adapt to the unsettling situation of birth and to find postnatal equilibrium in the face of this crisis. "What the child is seeking instinctively (as opposed to consciously)," explains Loder, "is a center around which to integrate this multiplicity of new activities and emerging competencies."[22] The child is attempting to resolve her precariousness by employing new competencies like biting, grasping, or calling the caregiver back in order to control her environment. This attempt to deal with an existential problem (our precariousness and the possibility that we could not exist) by way of a functional solution (the employment of new competencies) fails the child, and the presence of a face (a person who is present) becomes an interpersonal center of focus.

Following Erik Erikson, Loder argues that in the caregiver's faithfulness, the foundation of future trust is being laid. However, there have been times when the face has been absent, and this absence has stimulated the fear of abandonment and has produced mistrust. Loneliness haunts us, and we long for an affirming presence, a sense of connectedness. As Loder explains, it is the face-to-face relationship that will overcome our loneliness and negation. The face-to-face relation is

21. Fulkerson, "A Place to Appear," p. 171.

22. James E. Loder, "Negation and Transformation: A Study in Theology and Human Development," *Toward Moral and Religious Maturity: The First International Conference on Moral and Religious Development* (Morristown, NJ: Silver Burdett, 1980), p. 170.

"prototypical" in that it "embodies both the process and ontology of religious experience." The negation of our sense of negation, that is to say, the transformational process that results in our having a sense of connectedness, is, in Loder's words, "affected by a cosmic ordering, self-confirming impact from the presence of a loving other."[23] What intellectual capacities are required for this to happen? I would argue, none. As I will argue in a later chapter, the act of offering oneself to another as a self-affirming presence, of electing another as a friend, is a way of participating in God's presence and is a way to offer adolescents with developmental disabilities the self-confirming impact from the presence of a loving other. One place that this should happen is in our congregations. Research suggests that it has not.

Spiritual Nomads

Erik Carter's critical and well-documented evaluation of congregational life is that faith communities have been largely inhospitable to persons with developmental disabilities, erecting barriers to full participation, whether architectural, attitudinal, communicative, or programmatic. Consequently, such persons do not encounter the community life, relationships, and spiritual growth that people without disabilities experience in faith communities.[24] He has noted that even if adolescents with disabilities do attend worship (for which there is a 13 to 20 percent "participation gap" between people with and without disabilities), "only 14% participated in other congregational activities, such as youth groups and choirs."[25] Professor of Special Education and blogger Jeff McNair appeals to a *Joni and Friends* study that suggests 95 percent of people with disabilities do not attend church![26]

After an intriguing (though not ethnically diverse — quantitatively small in scope and not longitudinal) study on the use of religion in coping with the stressors associated with having a child with autism, Tarakeshwar and Pargament came to the following conclusion: "As a

23. Loder, "Negation and Transformation," p. 173.

24. Erik W. Carter, *Including People with Disabilities in Faith Communities: A Guide for Service Providers, Families, and Congregations* (Baltimore: Paul H. Brookes, 2007), pp. 6-16.

25. Carter, *Including People with Disabilities*, p. 7.

26. Jeff McNair, *The Church and Disability: The weblog disabledChristianity* (Jeff McNair, 2009), p. 165.

negative aspect of religion unique to autism, some parents reported distress because of their child's inability to remain quiet during church services. It appears that the insensitivity of the church toward the challenges of raising an autistic child caused a strain on being able to function as a family. In fact, 30% of the parents who were interviewed reported discontent with their clergy and church members."[27] Their research can easily be confirmed anecdotally. Jeff McNair agrees that churches have been complicit in perpetuating and affirming a culture that stigmatizes and excludes those persons with disabilities. He argues, "Normality is also reflected in our church structures. How else could you have the major weekly meeting of the church be something that is so social skill intensive? Our structures not only reflect normality they then enforce normality, in a relatively constrained way. That is, it doesn't take much in terms of difference for you to stand out at church."[28] Consequently, parents report receiving more support from their personal beliefs and spirituality than from any congregation or organized religion. The churches simply aren't there for them, leaving them to be spiritual nomads.

But there are further problems.

Aside from the obvious problem that the church is complicit in perpetuating unjust social structures and the theological issue that the entire body of Christ is not being represented, there are many benefits of religious faith and belonging to a faith community for the general population that people with disabilities are being excluded from. Some include "greater longevity, better management of stress and crises, and the experiencing of a greater sense of meaning and purpose in one's life."[29] Faith communities offer places for people with disabilities to experience social roles, a way to understand themselves beyond pathological self-definitions or medical understandings, and a place to develop social relationships and a sense of belonging and connectedness. This sense of validation and belonging mitigates the hopelessness of loneliness.

27. Nalini Tarakeshwar and Kenneth I. Pargament, "Religious Coping in Families of Children with Autism," *Focus on Autism and Other Developmental Disabilities* 16, no. 4 (Winter 2001): 256.

28. McNair, *The Church and Disability*, p. 154.

29. Jeannine Vogel, Edward A. Polloway, and J. David Smith, "Inclusion of People with Mental Retardation and Other Developmental Disabilities in Communities of Faith," *Mental Retardation* 44, no. 2 (April 2006): 111.

The Need for a New Approach to Ministry

There are certainly some congregations that have welcomed and incorporated the nearly 20 percent who have been dissed, labeled, and are facing an aching emptiness as spiritual nomads — but they are few in number. There are some parachurch groups that have. There is at least one parachuch group that has begun to reach out to adolescents with disabilities as part of a comprehensive strategy of evangelism to adolescents, but they are still negotiating how time spent with people with disabilities might challenge them to rearticulate their theological standards and norms for the practice of evangelistic ministry. The ministry to people with disabilities is still an appendix or shoulder ministry. Our congregations don't need a program for reaching "the disabled" — we need a new approach to congregational ministry that includes and amplifies the witness of our friends with developmental disabilities.

chapter 3

Affirming Presence
....
Imago Dei

"Off-Duty Image of God" versus
"God's Face Is the Face of the Retarded"

"I Did It!"

"I did it! I did it!" Jeff was so excited that he had conquered his fears and taken on the challenge of the high ropes course, forty feet above the ground. "I did it!" does not, however, communicate the entire story. Jeff has ASD and has a very difficult time communicating, but he clearly communicated to me that he was up for an adventure. At this summer camp, kids come with "buddies," typically developing friends from home who, together with the camp staff, ensure that kids with special needs can attempt anything they are willing to do. For Jeff and me, this meant that I helped Jeff put on his harness and move his lobster claws from element to element, and I partnered with him throughout the course.

The first "element" is the entrance to the course. Campers launch from a hillside platform across twenty-five feet of thin wire to a platform on a tree where they begin the course. Jeff headed out first, visibly nervous but committed to accomplishing this feat. I followed closely behind, and all was well until Jeff looked down. Jeff had more faith in me than in his harness, and consequently climbed onto me for safety. Since we were closer to the platform leading to the first element than the platform from which we started, I pushed ahead wearing my frontal Jeff harness. When we finally arrived at a sturdy surface, I convinced Jeff to dismount me. My hands had deep impressions from where I had grasped the crosswire for support. I tried to convince Jeff to continue, but he was not interested. He had accomplished his goal and was ready to return.

After asking the course attendants for thick leather gloves, I allowed Jeff to mount me again and we returned. We were both a little shaken and out of breath, so we found a comfortable low-lying bench from which we shared a drink and a snack and watched others conquer their fears at the ropes course challenge. After a while Jeff looked at me and said, "Thanks . . . call parents." I asked him, "What are your parents going to say?" and he quickly responded with a fist thrust in the air. "Proud. I did it! I did it!" Yes Jeff, you did it. And I have the scars to prove it.

Jeff is at ease with his interdependence. Despite the fact he rode me most of the way, he did accomplish his adventure course goals. While Jeff is lacking certain intellectual and social capacities that would allow him to go to college, hold most jobs, or articulate his faith in a coherent and cogent fashion, he does understand relationships and interdependence in a way that many of us never will. Jeff has an important contribution to make to our understanding of the image of God.

"Off-Duty Image of God"

A prominent theologian has described people like Jeff with the phrase, "off-duty image of God."[1] This viewpoint is understandable only if one's notion of the image of God has been dominated by concepts like reason, self-consciousness, moral freedom, the ability to create, purposive agency, or some other feature or capacity that is understood to be intrinsic to human nature. Consider the following reflection by Orthodox scholar Timothy Ware: "The image, or to use the Greek term the *icon,* of God signifies our human free will, our reason, our sense of

---

1. Jürgen Moltmann quoting Helmut Thielicke, cited in Brett Webb-Mitchell, *Unexpected Guests at God's Banquet: Welcoming People with Disabilities into the Church* (New York: Crossroad, 1994), p. 15.

moral responsibility — everything, in short, which marks us out from the animal creation and makes each of us a person."[2] If Ware and others are correct about what comprises the image of God, then persons who lack such capacities can only reflect God imperfectly or as images of a lesser God.

It would be nice if scholars could give us more direction for just exactly what the image of God is in Scripture. Without getting into the debates, what can be stated is that biblical scholars get weighed down in technical, though important, arguments about etymology (the origins of words and historical development of their meaning) and the author's intention in employing those words. Their conclusions are often very measured statements, like, "Given what we have noted about the poetic parallelism, number, gender, and definiteness expressed in the account of Gen 1:26-28 . . . [we can say that] Both the individual human being and humankind in its differentiated collectivity are related to the image of God."[3] Good starting point, but more needs to be said.

Paul Sands injects the notion of vocation into the discussion of the image of God and comes to the following conclusion: "In a remarkable 'democratization' of the imago Dei concept, Genesis 1 indicates that all humans — not just rulers or other elites — are called to mediate God's presence, power, and rule in the earth."[4] This view certainly opens the door for persons with developmental disabilities to be included in our conception of the image of God. Sands offers us a helpful way to talk about the image of God in a way that accounts for the diversity of creation. In a way similar to Sands, Pentecostal scholar Amos Yong, in his *Theology and Down Syndrome*, emphasizes the democratic nature of the Spirit by developing a concept he identifies as the "pneumatological imagination." The pneumatological imagination challenges us to consider the relationship between unity and diversity in the action of the Spirit and alerts us to "seek out, listen to, and discern the presence and activity of the Holy Spirit" in the tongues of the disabled.[5] Adolescents with developmental disabilities are indeed image bearers.

2. Timothy Ware, *The Orthodox Church* (New York: Penguin Books, 1997), p. 219.

3. Paul Niskanen, "The Poetics of Adam: The Creation of אדם in the Image of אלהים," *Journal of Biblical Literature* 128, no. 3 (2009): 435.

4. Paul Sands, "The *Imago Dei* as Vocation," *Evangelical Quarterly* 82, no. 1 (2010): 37.

5. Amos Yong, *Theology and Down Syndrome: Reimagining Disability in Late Modernity* (Waco, TX: Baylor University Press, 2007), p. 13.

If our conception of the image of God cannot account for the reality of adolescents with developmental disabilities, then we should revisit our theological constructions in light of our experience and Scripture and reform our doctrine. For example, Stanley Hauerwas has famously stated:

> God's face is the face of the retarded; God's body is the body of the retarded; God's being is that of the retarded. For the God we Christians must learn to worship is not a god of self-sufficient power, a god who in self-possession needs no one; rather ours is a God who needs a people, who needs a son. Absoluteness of being or power is not a work of the God we have come to know through the cross of Christ.[6]

John Swinton agrees with Hauerwas in this regard and argues that disabilities are not illnesses to be eradicated or overcome, they are alternative ways of living in the world — "authentic forms of human existence which reveal something of the image of God."[7]

How one understands the image of God has implications for one's practice of ministry. For example, out of her experience of being a chaplain to people with intellectual disabilities, Tracy Demmons argues that such persons are often excluded from the types of pastoral care that sustain most Christians and those forms of pastoral care for which most seminarians are trained. She argues that the lack of self-awareness and inability to think abstractly in the intellectually disabled make occasional visitation, offering certain forms of prayer, and scriptural counsel ineffective as means of pastoral care. Grounded in a relational understanding of the image of God that is founded on Barth's notion of "being in encounter," she advocates the following approach:

> The form of care suggested differs from traditional care in that it does not emphasize support and care for the other — from the caregiver to patient. Rather this form of care focuses on care as friend-

---

6. Stanley Hauerwas, *Suffering Presence: Theological Reflections on Medicine, the Mentally Handicapped, and the Church* (Notre Dame: University of Notre Dame Press, 1986), p. 178.

7. John Swinton, "Building a Church for Strangers," *Journal of Religion, Disability & Health* 4, no. 4 (2001): 48.

ship — both the caregiver and the care receiver give and receive in relationship.[8]

Such insights are important for those wishing to minister to and with adolescents with developmental disabilities. If the image of God is more about relationality than a certain type of rationality, then the way we approach discipleship and Christian education, not just for people with disabilities, but also for all people, must be informed by this reality. Demmons's conclusion follows, "Persons with intellectual disabilities may be unable to conceive of abstract concepts, such as God and time, but are fully able to encounter the other."[9] As I will develop below, a practice-centered approach to discipleship together with a focus on the practice of friendship is one way to reach adolescents with developmental disabilities where they live.

Friendship

"Deodorant and Discipleship"

You may not think the two are related — let me tell you how they are. Greg is a volunteer leader with a ministry to adolescents with developmental disabilities. He has been hanging out with Gibson and Wesley for two years now. At first he was frustrated with Wesley, an overweight, occasionally effluvious, overbearing bully (not the mean-spirited variety, but a bully nonetheless) who rarely took responsibility for himself or his actions. You would not believe this description if you saw Wesley today. He recently accompanied me to a conference where he gave advice to a room full of interested volunteers with a prominent youth ministry organization about how to minister to and with people like himself. Wesley's conversion has transformed him from a selfish consumer to a servant leader — for example, where his primary concern used to be to get as much food for himself at our meetings as he could, during one of our recent events he purchased and brought gluten-free

---

8. Tracy Demmons, "Embodied Encounter Through Imagination and the Arts: Toward a (Barthian) Theology and Praxis of Pastoral Care and Counseling for Persons with Intellectual Disabilities," *Journal of Religion, Disability and Health* 12, no. 4 (2008): 366.

9. Demmons, "Embodied Encounter," p. 367.

snacks for Franklin because he knew Franklin had a restricted diet and might feel left out. Wesley's conversion is an ongoing process that has occurred in the context of a community of faith. One of the most significant factors in Wesley's continuing conversion was the fact that Greg cared enough about him to tell him to stop eating chips by the bag, soda by the two-liter bottle, and fast food from the supersize menu. Greg also alerted him to the fact that whatever he was doing for hygiene was not sufficient. Wesley had, I'm sure, heard this from others. But, he had never heard it from someone who deeply cared for him, had his best interests in mind, and had proven that he loved him over the course of time. Wesley, of course, responded; and this little change has made a huge difference in his self-confidence and in how he is perceived by his mainstream peers.

Along the same lines, Gibson is prone to make huge claims. He has a fierce competitive spirit inside a frail body with cerebral palsy. Usually when people hear Gibson's claims they ignore him. Greg, however, made him account for his claims. Greg explained to me that no one takes Gibson seriously enough; no one values his opinion or thoughts enough to engage him — they are content to let him get away with outlandish claims and to let him never own up to his mistakes, and in this way are complicit in his marginalization. Greg values Gibson enough to correct him. It is no wonder they are best friends.

Academic studies have demonstrated that friendship has many benefits to adolescents with developmental disabilities. One study, citing contemporary researchers, concludes that "high-quality friendships are associated with positive school attitudes and can lessen the likelihood of being victimized by peers."[10] After reviewing recent studies on the impact of friendship and how they mitigate feelings of rejection or loneliness, the study concludes, "the extant literature suggests that close friendships are a key factor to students' success in school and subsequent functioning as young adults." And, furthermore, "Having even a single friend has been shown to reduce the impact of general peer rejection."[11] Friendship is the Christian practice that addresses the fundamental need we have to be connected.

10. David B. Estell, Martin H. Jones, Ruth Pearl, and Richard van Acker, "Best Friendships of Students with and without Learning Disabilities Across Late Elementary School," *Exceptional Children* 76, no. 1 (Fall 2009): 110.

11. Estell et al., "Best Friendships," p. 111.

Friendship shows a way of relating to a person with developmental disabilities beyond the medical model of care — an etiology, signs and symptoms, or a technical solution to the "problem" of disability. In the medical model, disability is often characterized in a way similar to an illness; a specific, definable pathology and an individual problem to be eliminated — this model does not address the human, as such. It also does not account for the social setting of the problem or society's complicity in the larger problem (stigmatization, alienation, oppression, exclusion). Friendship changes the relationship: *"The priority of friends,"* John Swinton reminds us, *"is the personhood of the other and not the illness."*[12] Christian friendship — the affirming presence of another — transcends relational boundaries of likeness, instrumentality, or social exchange.

Friendship in Historical Perspective

The classic Ciceronian expression of friendship reserves true friendship for educated males who share common virtues. In Homer, friendship is evoked by the attraction of like to like; in Hesiod friendship is reserved for those who are friendly toward you or who provide a relationship that is useful in some way; Aristotle introduced a broader view of friendship that includes wishing well for the other for the other's sake, but he still limits friendship to the consciously mutual. For Aristotle, therefore, friendship with gods is impossible because they are too remote and superior.[13]

Historically, we can discern many types of instrumental friendships, friendships for advantage or pleasure, but, speaking in terms of Christian practices, these never reach excellence because the partners do not love each other for the sake of each other but instead invest in each other for some benefit. In its classical expression the possibility of extending friendship to "tax-collectors and sinners" is inconceivable. As Bill Gaventa summarizes,

---

12. John Swinton, *Resurrecting the Person: Friendship and the Care of People with Mental Health Problems* (Nashville: Abingdon, 2000), p. 37, emphasis his.

13. Liz Carmichael, *Friendship: Interpreting Christian Love* (London: T. & T. Clark, 2004), p. 16.

At the risk of being too simplistic, one could summarize the classical philosophical view of friendship as important because it was necessary for an understanding of universal values and truth. In the biblical tradition, friendship reveals the grace, love, and call of a caring God. In the classical view, friendship was a human pathway to the universal or divine. In the biblical tradition, it is a pathway of the divine to humankind, a gift of grace that calls for human response.[14]

If friendship is a "gift of grace" that is freely given to another without the expectation of some reciprocal benefit, then the way is opened for authentic friendships with those on the margins of society. In an act of grace, one can simply choose another as friend regardless of any consideration of social benefit or promotion in social status.

Following Gaventa's logic, election is at the heart of the Christian practice of friendship. Christian friendship demands that we follow God in electing the other as friend by grace and that we allow room for their response. Of course, just because I open myself to friendship with a student with developmental disabilities does not mean that he will receive my friendship! He can choose to reject me. There is both a choosing and a being chosen in friendship. Electing another as a friend can lead to some "unlikely alliances."

Unlikely Alliances

Historically, one important part of the movement for disability rights has been deinstitutionalization, a process that made it possible for people with intellectual disabilities to enter into the kind of relationships with others that make the development of a different kind of identity possible. According to Amos Yong, it was important when the process of deinstitutionalization began, as it is vitally important now, that "this new paradigm emphasized social services, professional support networks, and most importantly, the cultivation of *genuine friendships*."[15] O'Brien and O'Brien call relationships between persons with

14. Bill Gaventa, "Gift and Call: Recovering the Spiritual Foundations of Friendships," *Friendships and Community Connections between People with and without Developmental Disabilities*, ed. Angela Novak Amado (Baltimore: Paul H. Brookes, 1993), p. 45.

15. Yong, *Theology and Down Syndrome*, p. 57.

and without disabilities "unlikely alliances." In their estimation, sustained relationships between persons with developmental disabilities and those without rarely form outside of family or social service settings.[16] This conclusion is not acceptable for a church that is called to befriend those on the margins of society. As the body of Christ, we need to be guided by a more complete vision of the *imago Dei* and challenged in response to reevaluate our relationships.

Relationships as Sacramental, Not Instrumental

Too often people choose to "reach out" to people with disabilities as a "ministry" or "service project." When the program or project has ended, the encounter is on hold until the next meeting. There is a goal beyond the personal encounter of the other that makes our relationships instrumental to some other end (the success of the program or ministry, the goal of becoming a church that is perceived as being inclusive, the stimulation of personal feelings of satisfaction that issue from knowing we have transgressed boundaries, etc.). Relationships can't be instrumental to the success of a program or to feelings of personal satisfaction. I confess that relationships are sacramental.

Karl Barth scholar Eberhard Busch, while expounding the implications of Barth's "the church as witness" ecclesiology, notes Barth's de-sacramentalization of the sacraments. The "sacraments" for Barth are primarily human, though "subordinate and reactive," responses to the prevenient action, or initiative of God.[17] Quoting a discussion between Barth and ministers from the Rhineland, Busch offers the following words from Barth on the subject:

> What we need is an energetic desacramentalizing of the church. . . . We must learn to understand that our thinking and speaking and doing, yes, also our cultic doing, including baptism and Lord's Supper, are *human responses* to God's Word and not a peculiar mixture of divine and human things. [We must learn that we] take our

16. John O'Brien and Connie Lyle O'Brien, "Unlikely Alliances: Friendships and People with Developmental Disabilities," in Amado, ed., *Friendships and Community Connections between People with and without Developmental Disabilities,* p. 10.

17. Craig Carter, "Karl Barth's Revision of Protestant Ecclesiology," *Perspectives in Religious Studies* 22 (2001): 41.

place with modesty: not as gods or half-gods, but in full responsibility before God.[18]

Why mention Barth's tendency toward "energetic desacramentalization"? Because against his strong language about de-sacramentalizing the traditionally understood sacraments, his language about the neighbor as sacramentally significant is intensified.

Barth argues that in seeing the other who is without hope, the potential neighbor, the "afflicted fellow-man," we see a mirror. Through the spectacles of redemption, as those who know that they belong to God, we see that without God's grace and the power of an active God we would be that afflicted person. Jesus, in solidarity and identity with us, confronts us in a revelatory way when he crosses our path as that neighbor. As Barth explains,

> Jesus Christ is always concealed in the neighbour. The neighbour is not a second revelation of Jesus Christ side by side with the first. When he meets me, the neighbour is not in any sense a second Christ. He is only my neighbour. And it is only as such and in his difference from Christ, only as a sign instituted by Christ, that we can speak of his solidarity and identity with Christ.[19]

The neighbor, while not "a second Christ," does have the capacity to be a vehicle of God's grace or, in Newbigin's phrasing, to be a sign, instrument, and foretaste of the grace of God. Therefore, if I am a disciple of Christ, again, in Barth's words:

> I will therefore willingly and joyfully accept what the neighbour has to show me, because I am actually in need of it. Whether willingly and wittingly or not, in showing it, *my neighbour acquires for me a sacramental significance.* In this capacity he becomes and is a visible sign of invisible grace, a proof that I, too, am not left alone in this world, but am borne and directed by God.[20]

---

18. Eberhard Busch, "Karl Barth's Understanding of the Church as Witness," *Saint Luke's Journal of Theology* 33, no. 2 (March 1990): 92.

19. Karl Barth, *Church Dogmatics*, II/1: *The Doctrine of God*, ed. G. W. Bromiley and T. F. Torrance (Edinburgh: T. & T. Clark, 1957), p. 435.

20. Barth, *Church Dogmatics*, II/1, p. 436.

In even stronger language the Gospel of Matthew describes parabolically the identification of God with his children when it states, "just as you did it to one of the least of these who are members of my family, you did it for me" (Matt. 25:40). When we recognize that every encounter with the neighbor is a divine appointment, we will be more attentive to his presence and more receptive to the presence of others.

Fireworks

It was a lazy summer late afternoon at the river. Every family brought a side dish and I had cooked the hotdogs ahead of time so I could be present with the kids when they arrived. The big activity was riding on a boat, and some had the opportunity to be pulled behind the boat on a tube. Kids welcomed friends. Jarod's mother stated, "He has other places where people greet him, but he is only himself when he is with the group. He doesn't worry about not fitting in. He is relaxed. He is Jarod."

Peter did not want to have anything to do with the boat. He sat alone on the shore. I joined him and we sat together on the shore throwing rocks into the water. "Fireworks!" Peter shouted. I had no idea what he was talking about. "We aren't going to have fireworks tonight," I explained. "Maybe on the Fourth of July," I added, not wanting to disappoint him. "Fireworks!" he insisted as he threw another handful of rocks into the river and pointed. And, he was right; the splashes from the rocks did look like fireworks. I was throwing rocks into a river, but Peter was making fireworks.

When I tried to see things from his perspective, when I took the time necessary to slow down, be present, watch, and listen, I too was able not only to see the fireworks, but also to invite people to join in the pleasure of making fireworks. This anecdote is not about seeing fireworks; it is about reconsidering our relationships, connecting with others, and place-sharing.

Place-Sharing

I get the term "place-sharing" from Andy Root's *Revisiting Relational Youth Ministry*. Root builds on Dietrich Bonhoeffer's approach to ethics to make the case that relationships, according to the model of the humanity of Jesus Christ, require that we take responsibility for the other and stand with him or her as an advocate. As Root describes it, "Bonhoeffer holds that the concrete place of God's revelation (the place where God reveals Godself and is present to us) is within personal encounter, shared relational bonds of *I* and the *other*."[21] Place-sharing is not instrumental to some other goal, like evangelizing another, but is a reflection of the place-sharing God. Bonhoeffer recognizes that place-sharing with the neighbor has a revelatory, sacramental aspect. Root quotes Bonhoeffer scholar Clifford Green to make his point: "God's transcendence is not remote otherness or absence; God's otherness is embodied precisely in the other person who is real and present, encountering me in the heart of my existence with the judgment and grace of the gospel."[22]

As this relates to the approach to ministry presented in this book, place-sharing is a form of affirming presence, a way of spiritual friendship — a practice that creates a space in which an encounter with the living Lord occurs. Since place-sharing emphasizes taking responsibility for the other, and some people have limitations that make them require more care, place-sharing can be asymmetrical. The practice of friendship creates a space in which persons with developmental disabilities can experience the spiritual reality of being connected to God and others. This friendship is not utilitarian or instrumental to some other goal, but is simply sharing life together in such a way that the unique humanity of adolescents with developmental disabilities is affirmed in our relationship and they are afforded a new identity — friend.

> Through the practice of spiritual friendship, a person with profound learning disabilities is no longer a member of an amorphous group — "the mentally handicapped" — excluded and alienated from sources of value and positive self-worth. Rather, in and through the gift of friendship, the learning disabled are enabled to develop a new identity as "persons in relation" with whom others desire to relate and are prepared to strive to find ways of relating, which operate beyond the boundaries of cognition and intellect.[23]

21. Andrew Root, *Revisiting Relational Youth Ministry: From a Strategy of Influence to a Theology of Incarnation* (Downers Grove, IL: InterVarsity, 2007), p. 107.

22. Root, *Revisiting Relational Youth Ministry*, p. 140.

23. John Swinton and Esther McIntosh, "Persons in Relation: The Care of Persons with Learning Disabilities," *Theology Today* 57, no. 2 (2000): 184.

This kind of relationship won't happen unless someone takes the initiative to make it happen.

Elected to Friendship

Unless I pursue Andrew, we will not have a relationship. I must place myself where I can respond to his initiative and allow him to be a host. He is an adolescent with a very limited social network and no means of transportation, aside from his parents. If we are to become friends, it will not be because I have taken forays into his life that have allowed my life to remain untouched. To elect to be his friend moves me beyond a comfortable and unimposing friendship. Election is the theological motivation that moves me to cross boundaries. While Andrew's capacity for self-representation is as weak as his voice, he has many treasures to share in the mutuality of a friendship — even if the friendship requires my constant initiative. I recognize that having Andrew as a friend is not an option; I need Andrew. In this sense, our relationship is characterized by mutuality.

Mutuality is expressed in the voluntary nature of friendship. Disabilities studies specialist Zana Lutfiyya explains, "The knowledge that another person wants to be with one, spend time and do things together out of affection or by choice is a powerful affirmation of one's worth and value."[24] Family connections are of natural necessity or obligation, and service-client relationships are based on a contract. A full sense of belonging requires one's being chosen. Ethicist Hans Reinders focuses the issue of being chosen theologically and adds that developing friendship with others is a vocational calling:

> I wish to confront the longstanding convictions in the Christian tradition with implications of exclusion that have never been properly questioned. . . . Every human being is worthy of being chosen as a friend simply because that is what God does — choose us to be friends. . . . [F]riendship with fellow creatures is our vocation.[25]

24. Zana Marie Lutfiyya, "'A Feeling of Being Connected': Friendships between People with and without Learning Difficulties," *Disability, Handicap and Society* 6, no. 3 (1991): 240.

25. Hans S. Reinders, *Receiving the Gift of Friendship: Profound Disability, Theological Anthropology, and Ethics* (Grand Rapids: Eerdmans, 2008), p. 62.

Our co-humanity with others and God's initiative in choosing us as friends irrespective of our worth are important aspects of the doctrine of election. We are all united in our unworthy status before God; we are all receivers of grace. God elects us to friendship together. Newbigin's reflections on the doctrine of election are helpful as we consider how we are all connected and need one another. Newbigin argues,

> If each human being is to be ultimately understood as an independent spiritual monad, then salvation could only be through an action directed impartially to each and all. But if the truly human is the shared reality of mutual and collective responsibility that the Bible envisages, then salvation must be an action that binds us together and restores for us the true mutual relation to each other and the true shared relation to the world of nature.[26]

At the heart of the doctrine of election is the belief that nobody makes friends with God; God makes friends with people. Put another way, "God has always been a friend for us, and his friendship precedes any of our actions. . . . If God's friendship were conditioned by our response, we would have lost his friendship long ago."[27] I believe that the doctrine of election can guide our thinking about friendship.

For example, studies have shown that children with autism who have the opportunity to develop "friendships" with typically developing peers were "more responsive to one another, had stronger receptive language skills, exhibited greater positive social interaction and cohesion, and demonstrated more complex coordinated play."[28] My issue with some of this research is the definition of "satisfactory friendship" as "an interpersonal achievement built upon a foundation of interpersonal skills (e.g., the child's ability to form affective bonding) and social cognitive skills (e.g., perspective taking — theory of mind)."[29] This definition of friendship excludes too many people. Christian friendship is a grace-filled offering that is not dependent on the responsive-

---

26. Lesslie Newbigin, *The Open Secret: An Introduction to the Theology of Mission* (Grand Rapids: Eerdmans, 1995), pp. 70-71.

27. Reinders, *Receiving the Gift of Friendship*, p. 297.

28. Nirit Bauminger et al., "Friendship in High-functioning Children with Autism Spectrum Disorder: Mixed and Non-mixed Dyads," *Journal of Autism and Developmental Disorders* 38 (2008): 1211.

29. Bauminger et al., "Friendship in High-functioning Children," p. 1211.

ness of the other. Christian friendship is about "election" — a choice. Such a choice can move people beyond the barriers of the lack of reciprocity; theory-of-mind deficits that betray a lack of understanding of others' emotions, feelings, and desires; and a seeming distance in affection. By the world's standards, it is the kids who are the most capable in terms of social skills, who are more verbal, have higher IQs, and can negotiate the complex rules of reciprocity that govern children's friendships who are more likely to have friends. This is, of course, friendship based on human capacities and affinity. This is friendship as if Jesus didn't matter. Friendship as election is based on a call.

> Call means believing that others may in fact commit themselves to a relationship and friendship in ways that defy explanation. It means operating from the framework that friendship is a covenant relationship, not a relationship characterized by giver-receiver or by the service system's reliance on "compliance with a code."[30]

"My Place"

My Place is a 5,100-square-foot, completely accessible playground that was built at our local Parks and Recreation Center. It is "a place to be me" that accommodates all children regardless of ability by providing a firm yet spongy surface that minimizes the consequence of falls, activities that are low enough and spaced such that they are accessible to all and require little physical effort to manipulate and enjoy. The problem is, without anyone to take kids there, it rarely fulfills that vision for which it was created. Accessibility is not enough. As Reinders explains,

> The practices and politics of inclusion will not create a lasting change for persons with disabilities unless there will be people willing to invest in friendships with them. Without true friendships, disabled persons will enjoy the new opportunities created by their equal rights most likely as "strangers in a strange land."[31]

Block argues that the Christian community must go beyond this type of accessibility. "Liberation and real access to the community," she

30. Gaventa, "Gift and Call," p. 60.
31. Reinders, *Receiving the Gift of Friendship*, p. 187.

explains, "will only be realized through personal relationships that develop into genuine friendships."[32] In fact, one important goal of community-based services for people with learning difficulties is to encourage relationships as a means to help people with disabilities be more assimilated into mainstream society. At the same time, there are limitations to programmatic efforts to forge voluntary relationships such as friendships. The propinquity that comes with accessibility does not ensure intimacy. One phenomenological study of friendships between people with and without disabilities yielded several findings that are of interest to our line of inquiry. Most importantly, the study highlighted the notion that mutuality in relationships — a web of activities and support, inspiration, and togetherness — can nurture a *"feeling of being connected."*[33] Friendship is the first practice in a ministry of affirming presence that can address the disconnected lives of so many adolescents with developmental disabilities.

Connected

My first impression of Galen immediately brought to mind the description of Dr. James Mortimer by Sir Arthur Conan Doyle in *The Hound of the Baskervilles:* "He had large, quivering fingers as agile and restless as the antennae of an insect."[34] While the logic of the antennae's movement is inscrutable to the observer, they are busily working to determine moisture, discern scents, taste surroundings, locate food, or detect enemies. Galen's motions are often as erratic to me, but I know they are purposeful. Galen has ASD, which in his case manifests itself physically through the typical repetitive motions and rituals (often involving glasses, wads of string, or cars that look like his parents' cars) and peculiar responses to the variety of sensory stimuli that are part of the wallpaper of our lives. He has severely impaired reciprocal interaction and, therefore, has had a difficult time entering into friendships. Consequently, Galen appears to be disconnected, at times, from relationships.

32. Jennie Weiss Block, *Copious Hosting: A Theology of Access for People with Disabilities* (New York: Continuum, 2002), p. 158.

33. Lutfiyya, "'A Feeling of Being Connected,'" p. 238.

34. Arthur Conan Doyle, "The Hound of the Baskervilles," in *The Complete Sherlock Holmes,* vol. 1 (New York: Barnes and Noble Classics, 2003), p. 579.

His mother recently gave him string for his birthday and he returned to her a look that communicated, "You get me, Mom. You really get me." Following her example, and in an effort to teach Galen prayer, we made prayer chains together — beads attached to string and anchored by a cross such that the beads can be slid from one end of the string chain to the other. Galen could take the string home with him and manipulate the string, which now had been sanctified (set apart for a holy purpose). Galen and I connected, and my prayer is that in the process of sharing that moment, Galen connected with God as well.

Connectedness is an expression of the spiritual dimension of life.[35] As Michael Buchanan, who has written extensively on religious education, has explained, "The spiritual has come to be understood in terms of the connectedness, or relationship an individual has with self, others, the world, and possibly with the Transcendent, named in the Christian tradition as God."[36] Buchanan adduces Marian de Souza's notion of spirituality, which can be seen as "relational, . . . demonstrated through the individual's expressions of connectedness to the human and non-human world."[37] De Souza, who has researched, consulted, and published extensively in the area of children's spirituality and education, has made the concept of the spiritual as "connectedness" central to her approach:

> My subsequent research was inspired by Nye's . . . notion of "relational consciousness" and it led me to my current understanding of spirituality, that it is a vital element of the human condition which pertains to human relationality whereby the individual experiences different levels of connectedness to Self and everything other than self. The latter includes connectedness to the Social and Communal Other, to the Physical Other in the world and to a Transcendent Other, and it is these relationships that invigorate and animate the individual's life as s/he moves forward on her/his spiritual journey. The movement comprises an outward motion to

35. Michael T. Buchanan, "The Spiritual Dimension of Curriculum Change," *International Journal of Children's Spirituality* 14, no. 4 (November 2009): 385.

36. Michael T. Buchanan, "Learning beyond the Surface: Engaging the Cognitive, Affective and Spiritual Dimension within the Curriculum," *International Journal of Children's Spirituality* 13, no. 4 (November 2008): 312.

37. Buchanan, "Learning beyond the Surface," pp. 312-13.

embrace others who are familiar, then moving on to connect to others who are different and unknown.[38]

The idea of being connected to others is an important yet underappreciated element of the biblical healing narratives. Many of the stories about Jesus healing people with disabilities and illness also include Jesus restoring to life-giving community a person who was once excluded from such communities. For example, in Luke 13:10-17 Jesus heals a woman described as having been "crippled" for eighteen years. There are many points to be made about this story, but the important one for our purposes is that she enters the synagogue a "crippled" woman and departs "a daughter of Abraham." Similarly, in Mark 5:21-43 when a woman is healed of a stigmatizing issue of blood by secretly touching the hem of Jesus' garment, Jesus not only allows her to give voice to her witness by offering him an account of the miracle, he restores her to community by publicly declaring her healed. In Luke 5:12-16 and 17:11-19, when lepers call to Jesus begging for pity, Jesus does not merely heal them; he allows them to act on their faith by going to priests in order to be declared clean, and in doing so, he furthermore restores them to the community by making sure the Mosaic requirement for being declared clean is met. These connections were a vital part of the healing ministry of Jesus. While there is much discussion from within the disability community as to whether healing, in the sense of cure or "fixing" the impairment, is even desirable,[39] there is no question that we are called to follow Jesus' model of healing as restoration to community and a sense of connectedness. For adolescents with developmental disabilities, this means helping them form relationships with their peers.

Peers

I had been corresponding with Amy's mother about another issue when I realized that she was about to have a birthday party and that only one

---

38. Marian de Souza, "Editorial: Spirituality and Well Being," *International Journal of Children's Spirituality* 14, no. 3 (August 2009): 181.

39. While cancer can be eliminated without eliminating the subject, many developmental disabilities, such as ASD, cannot. Is there an ideal Galen behind the autistic one I know?

or two friends would be attending. I immediately called as many high school kids as I could and invited them to join me at Amy's party. The kids and their parents responded and brought enormous energy to the party. Amy's mother was visibly moved by the gesture. Why is it important that Amy celebrate her birthday with her peers? Why is it so bad that Edward sits alone at a lunch table made to hold sixteen?

The intimacy of peer friendship is extremely important for socioemotional adaptation and for mitigating feelings of loneliness.[40] While for most adolescents peer relationships emerge naturally, for adolescents with developmental disabilities such relationships remain elusive. Carter and Pesko point to research that suggests that adolescents with more severe disabilities engage in few interactions with their mainstream peers and have few "durable friendships."[41] The conception of "durable" friendships is paramount. What is a durable friendship? It is a friendship that is able to withstand wear and pressure and that is lasting, enduring, and permanent. Unfortunately, adolescents with developmental disabilities have fewer settings available to them in which such friendships can develop. For example, not only do adolescents with disabilities engage in fewer social, recreational, and leisure activities, when they do participate in such activities they do so primarily with parents or other adults. What they are missing is the context in which to develop peer-to-peer relationships, and therefore the friendship development that typically developing children experience.[42]

Carter recognizes that students with disabilities have limited opportunities to develop relationships with their typically developing, general education peers. Carter, therefore, advocates a peer buddy program that allows for peers, rather than teachers or paid adult educational assistants, to provide in-school support for adolescents with disabilities. The encounter benefits the students with disabilities by providing opportunities to develop age-appropriate social skills with

40. J. G. Parker and S. R. Asher, "Friendship and Friendship Quality in Middle Childhood: Links with Peer Group Acceptance and Feelings of Loneliness and Social Dissatisfaction," *Developmental Psychology* 29 (1993): 611-21.

41. Erik W. Carter and Matthew J. Pesko, "Social Validity of Peer Interaction Intervention Strategies in High School Classrooms: Effectiveness, Feasibility, and Actual Use," *Exceptionality* 16 (2008): 156-57.

42. Abbie Solish, Adrienne Perry, Patricia Minnes, "Participation of Children with and without Disabilities in Social, Recreational and Leisure Activities," *Journal of Applied Research in Intellectual Disabilities* 23, no. 3 (May 2010): 226-36.

peers, expanded opportunities for encounters with other peers as a result of the new relationship, increased self-confidence to engage in other high school activities, and a safe place to try out new interpersonal skills. For example, adolescents with learning disabilities generally aren't cognizant of how their behavior impacts others, can't interpret the emotions and intentions of others and, accordingly, have difficulty recognizing or knowing how to resolve conflict. Such skills are essential to developing enduring or "durable" friendships. In peer buddy programs, the general education peers get the opportunity to know students who are different from them whom they otherwise would not have personally encountered and, consequently, increased diversity in their relationships, which contributes to the personal growth that obtains with being exposed to human differences and similarities.[43]

Carter recognizes that as the complexity of adolescent relationships increases in high school, without intentional, well-designed support strategies "students with severe disabilities may be physically integrated but not socially integrated among their peers without disabilities."[44] In fact, adolescents with severe disabilities are among the most isolated of all students.[45] Daniel and Warren were in the band, but often seemed peripheral and were dressed differently (almost as jesters or clowns — unlike the rest of the band who wore typical band uniforms). Jarod was on the football team, but he often stood alone on the sideline with his helmet on, not included in many of the celebrations or words of encouragement that occur throughout a game. Both boys are present, but only marginally included in the lives of their peers. Do any of the students on the football team or the band call them during the week or see them on the weekend?

In school, adult supports are the most frequently used means of student support; however, adult supports may actually hinder students from full participation in learning opportunities at school. Peer supports, on the other hand, "have the expressed goal of increasing both access to the general education curriculum and facilitating social interactions in general education settings that might not otherwise occur in

43. Erik W. Carter et al., "High School Peer Buddies: A Win-Win Situation," *Teaching Exceptional Children* (September/October 2002): 17-18.

44. Erik W. Carter and Craig H. Kennedy, "Promoting Access to the General Curriculum Using Peer Support Strategies," *Research and Practice for Persons with Severe Disabilities* 31, no. 4 (2006): 284.

45. Carter and Kennedy, "Promoting Access to the General Curriculum," p. 287.

these contexts."[46] Social interactions and ad hoc learning experiences that occur throughout the day among peers are a vital part of the general education curriculum and are the essential element of religious education and spiritual formation. It is not enough to indoctrinate; students must participate, and this will take intentionality and forethought on the part of youth leaders.

Certainly this translates into religious education as well. Is it only the youth leader or adult helpers who work with the kids? Research has shown that "[w]hen working with peer supports, students with severe disabilities were the recipients of increased and more diverse social support behaviors, including emotional support, companionship, material aid, informational support, and assistance with decisions."[47] Peers are poised to give such support in a way that adults simply can't because adults belong only as strangers to the sociocultural reality that is high school culture. However, when peers take responsibility for one another they begin to change the culture of the school and have reported experiencing "substantive personal benefits, including greater appreciation of diversity, personal growth, raised expectations of their classmates with disabilities, new friendships, a sense of accomplishment, and the acquisition of new skills."[48]

The question is: How, if at all, do these relationships extend beyond the school day? The development of "durable relationships" requires more opportunities for exposure to one another and common participation in activities.[49] But if kids with disabilities and general education peers never cross paths, how will these relationships be forged? Furthermore, if the encounter occurs in a context in which the ability to negotiate the high school social world is vital, then our friends are lost. It is certainly possible for a church to execute a program that merely mimics and reproduces high school culture. A ministry that wants to be hospitable to adolescents with developmental disabilities will challenge typically developing kids to move beyond similarity and propinquity as a foundation for friendship to intentionality and election. Friendship is every bit as authentic when it is based on election

46. Carter and Kennedy, "Promoting Access to the General Curriculum," p. 285.
47. Carter and Kennedy, "Promoting Access to the General Curriculum," p. 288.
48. Carter and Kennedy, "Promoting Access to the General Curriculum," p. 289.
49. "Friendships tend to form around a variety of shared contexts, characteristics, and activities. Among the key factors driving friendship formation is propinquity — physical closeness." Estell et al., "Best Friendships," p. 112.

and a commitment to love. The doctrine of election, and the Spirit of God, can move us to overcome daily patterns that never put us in a place where we encounter someone with a disability.

An effective ministry with adolescents is part of a comprehensive program of congregational nurture. For example, the process of selecting peers as friends begins at an early age. In fact, "By third grade popular children tend to have almost exclusively nonrejected friends."[50] While kids with disabilities in late elementary school typically have a best friend, and often as many best friends as their able-bodied peers, most of their friends also have disabilities and they have fewer long-term friends or what we have been calling durable friendships. The trend toward excluding certain kids has been well established by high school; therefore a liberative action is needed if adolescents with developmental disabilities are going to be chosen as friends. If "late childhood marks the beginning of patterns of functions of friendships that will endure throughout adolescence and into adulthood," then where does that leave adolescents with developmental disabilities? Research suggests that inclusive environments, absent the relationships that provide social supports, do not foster social acceptance. It is possible to be integrated, to be included, and still not accepted.[51] Having a program or accessible structure in place is not enough. Creating a space is more than organizing activities or a room.

The prospect of people with developmental disabilities developing friendship is even less promising at the other end of the age spectrum. Middle-aged and older persons with disabling conditions, especially those who have been deinstitutionalized, have an even more significantly limited network of informal social relationships.[52] Loving Christians who seek out such persons and elect them to friendship are the solution. However, just because someone is elected to friendship, it does not mean that they will necessarily reciprocate.

50. Estell et al., "Best Friendships," p. 112.

51. D. B. Estell, M. H. Jones, R. Pearl, R. Van Acker, T. W. Farmer, and P. C. Rodkin, "Peer Groups, Popularity, and Social Preference: Trajectories of Social Functioning among Students with and without Learning Disabilities," *Journal of Learning Disabilities* 41 (2008): 5-14.

52. Christine Bigby, "Known Well by No-one: Trends in the Informal Social Networks of Middle-aged and Older People with Intellectual Disability Five Years after Moving to the Community," *Journal of Intellectual and Developmental Disability* 33, no. 2 (June 2008): 148-57.

Rejection: Coping with a Lack of Markers

Wesley called me to make sure I was aware he was not going to be able to attend the annual Valentine's Gala, a dance that is one of our ministry's hallmark events. He stressed that he had another commitment, a dance he was attending with his girlfriend, and so he would not be able to attend. Brady told one of his friends that our ministry is for high schoolers and teased his friend because she still enjoyed going — of course Brady had also really enjoyed being a part of it up until a few weeks ago. What is going on?

Child psychologist David Elkind can help us understand. While Elkind's work does not specifically address the issue of kids with developmental disabilities, Elkind does touch on issues that are of interest to our discussion. One of his most enduring theses is that the vanishing markers of transition from childhood to adulthood evidence the lack of a significant place for teenagers in our society. These markers (a mark on the wall that represents growth as a child, a bar or bat mitzvah or first communion that demonstrates a new kind of participation in the faith community, graduation from college that may mark the end of adolescence and entry into society, a promotion at work that recognizes a job well done) demonstrate socially and confirm in adolescents psychosocially a sense of growing, maturing, and developing. Emerging from one stage to another often comes with new privileges and responsibilities. An important aspect of this process is that "giving up old markers also helps the young person become aware of his or her progress toward maturity."[53] Leaving certain things behind is a way to imagine progress in one's life.

Elkind makes the argument that markers (clothing markers, admission to certain types of activities, markers related to the loss of innocence, attaining a certain image, or having a new relationship to authority) keep adolescents from an inappropriately full participation in the adult world that they are not prepared for developmentally and allow them the space in which they can make safe and age-appropriate decisions. This is an important point for those who minister to and with adolescents, especially in an age when communications technol-

---

53. David Elkind, *All Grown Up and No Place to Go: Teenagers in Crisis* (New York: Addison-Wesley, 1984), p. 94.

ogy and aggressive marketing to teens have erased many of the boundaries that Elkind addressed.

I argue, along the lines of Elkind's notion of social markers, that kids with developmental disabilities have fewer markers available to them with which to measure their progress. They think: I have graduated from high school, yet I am riding the bus to high school with people I know to be much younger than I. I am twenty-one but my parents need to sleep in the hotel room next door if I want to have a getaway with my friends. At sixteen I didn't get a driver's license. At eighteen I did not get invited to the homecoming dance. At twenty-one I can't go to the store to purchase alcohol. Why does Ryan want to show me that he brought cigarettes to a youth group meeting? Because he wants me to know that he is old enough to have them. The fact that his mother took them away from him only confuses or erases the potential marker. Is there a way that our ministry can provide spiritual markers for kids with developmental disabilities? Do kids "graduate" to something? How can meaningful ceremonies and reunions be used to mark achievements? We will revisit these questions in a later chapter.

The attempt on the part of the adolescent with developmental disabilities to find markers can be hurtful to watch, especially when your relationship with them represents a stage in life that they want to move beyond. This is a great opportunity to demonstrate faithfulness in a friendship — are you the father who has been on the lookout for the lost son who then runs to the son when he decides to return? Or, do you partner with them to find a new community for them to be a part of, thereby mitigating the potential tension of leaving? Could you celebrate their moving on with a ceremony and prayers and give them the opportunity to come back to tell the group about what they are currently doing? The discomfort brought to bear on a relationship by a lack of social markers is only one thing that makes friendship with adolescents with developmental disabilities inconvenient.

The Inconvenience of Friendship

When I asked Christine Pohl what she thought of an article I had written, she gave me the following advice: make sure to include the difficult aspects of working with kids with developmental disabilities or the article will lose credibility. In other words, she was encouraging me not to romanticize work with kids with developmental disabilities — relationships are difficult and friendships are messy. Their limitations are real and have social and physical consequences. The list below is in no way a complaint. It is simply a list of things you will need to consider if you plan to spend time with some of my friends:[54]

- If you are planning to get together with them, they will probably need help with transportation.
- You might have difficulty understanding them when they speak and you will need to ask them to repeat themselves several times. You might still never get it.
- You will need to move at a much slower pace than you are accustomed to when you go somewhere with them.
- They probably won't be attuned to your emotional needs or show much enthusiasm for your interests, concerns, or accomplishments.
- They probably won't get your jokes — but they might laugh anyway.
- They will have a difficult time emotionally if the activity you share together is altered from their expectations.
- They might attempt to run away or hide from you.
- They might bite you.
- They might take off their clothes.
- If you take them to the pool, they might say things like, "I shouldn't pee in the pool," leaving you wondering if they already have.
- If you ever write a book, they will probably never read it.
- If they have something on their mind, and have the capacity to call or text, they might call and text you (home, office, cell, and spouse) until they get a response.
- They might never appreciate the fact that you are trying to advocate on their behalf.
- If you share a meal together you will need to make sure they don't eat anything they shouldn't.

54. This is just a list that has the intention of introducing you to some of the difficulties in establishing friendships with kids with developmental disabilities. Everyone is different and these descriptions are of particular individuals, not of "a typical developmentally disabled person." I could write several pages about the blessing of knowing each person described below — I hope that is clear by now.

- If you go to a theme park together you might need to make sure they don't jump on anyone.
- If you take them to church, expect some confused and concerned looks from the congregation.
- If they spend the night at your house, it is possible that you will need to change their sheets if their diapers leak at night, help them wash themselves in the shower, organize and administer their medicines. . . .

The truth is that many kids with developmental disabilities can be very difficult to be around. In his autobiographical account of life with a brother with low-functioning autism, Karl Greenfeld concludes hopelessly, "there is nothing to be gained from loving Noah but those lessons in patience and service and generosity and selflessness."[55] In Karl's difficult experience, Noah is an obligation — "a force, murky, complicated, extending beyond his own physical vessel to every single area of our life and consciousness" but not someone who could be a friend.[56]

We assume friendship should not be difficult, inconvenient, or a source of tension. We often, unthinkingly, interpret friendship individually and almost therapeutically in terms of a weak vision of personal fulfillment. Friends serve us similar to the way the God of Moralistic Therapeutic Deism serves us. Christian Smith describes Moralistic Therapeutic Deism as a religiosity that is characterized by a moralistic approach to life that issues in a socially affable niceness, therapeutic benefits to its adherents that include a sense of subjective well-being, and a Deistic god who is not involved in daily affairs yet is available for times of crisis.[57] Such a view of God does not provide the theological rationale or vision to encourage one to initiate a relationship with individuals with developmental disabilities. The way society imagines disability combined with a shallow picture of friendship makes relationships between people with and without disabilities uncommon. The story of *missio Dei,* the ongoing redemptive mission of God, challenges Moralistic Therapeutic Deism: it places disability in a larger story of God's redemptive action and moves

55. Karl Taro Greenfeld, *Boy Alone: A Brother's Memoir* (New York: HarperCollins, 2009), p. 340.

56. Greenfeld, *Boy Alone,* p. 263.

57. Christian Smith, *Soul Searching: The Religious and Spiritual Lives of American Teenagers* (Oxford: Oxford University Press, 2005), pp. 162-71.

people to cross barriers in the interest of discovering Christ who is already at work. The story of *missio Dei* reminds us that when it comes to bearing witness to God's redemptive work no one is impaired.

chapter 4

Amplifying Our Witness

Missio Dei

> *"The splendor of the rose and the whiteness of the lily do not rob the little violet of its scent nor the daisy of its simple charm. If every tiny flower wanted to be a rose, spring would lose its loveliness."*

Thérèse of Lisieux

From Jesters to Gesturers

In *A History of Mental Retardation,* R. C. Scheerenberger appeals to Christopher Hibbert's account of social life in Florence under the influence of Cosimo de Medici and his progeny. Hibbert addresses the economic, political, social, and religious life in Florence, including the popes under the de Medici dynasty. According to Hibbert's account of Pope Leo X's grand dinners,

> [b]uffoons and jesters were nearly always to be found at his table where the guests were encouraged to laugh at their antics and at the cruel jokes which were played on them — as when, for instance, some half-witted, hungry dwarf was seen guzzling a plate of carrion covered in a strong sauce under the impression that he was being privileged to consume the finest fare.[1]

1. Christopher Hibbert in R. C. Scheerenberger, *A History of Mental Retardation* (Baltimore: Paul H. Brookes, 1983), pp. 33-34.

People with developmental disabilities were not the jesters who had political influence and were often prophetic voices of critique. They were the buffoons who weren't taken seriously, who were the butt of the jokes. The purpose of this chapter is to remind us that adolescents with developmental disabilities should not be viewed as jesters, or as people we have to find some place for in our churches so they don't bother people who are enjoying their own personal worship experience. Instead, they need to be encouraged and supported as gesturers; people who enact their faith as full members of the body of Christ. Perhaps we aren't sure what to do with adolescents with developmental disabilities in the church because we have forgotten the purpose of the church and the source of our power.

Missio Dei

Missio Dei theology, at its core, is an affirmation that God is the author of mission. Mission does not issue from historical accident, church initiative, or human agency. The church does not have a mission *per se;* the church participates in God's ongoing redemptive mission. The purpose of the church is to bear witness to and participate in God's ongoing redemptive mission in the world. As David Bosch has affirmed, "It is not the church which 'undertakes' mission; it is the *missio Dei* which constitutes the church."[2] Darrell Guder argues that the *missio Dei* concept offers important guidance to the North American church today.[3] I believe that *missio Dei* is a crucial theological concept for understanding the place of adolescents with developmental disabilities in our congregations.

For example, Guder maintains that *missio Dei* reminds the church of the mystery of God and the impossibility of defining or controlling divine revelation. From my perspective *missio Dei* confronts the church with the fact that able-ist theological traditions are not normative for the congregation that is the body of Christ. The body of Christ has developmental disabilities. Guder argues that *missio Dei* theology reminds

2. David J. Bosch, *Transforming Mission: Paradigm Shifts in Theology of Mission,* American Society of Missiology Series, no. 16 (Maryknoll, NY: Orbis, 1991), p. 519.

3. Darrell L. Guder, "The Missio Dei: A Mission Theology after Christendom," in *News of Boundless Riches: Interrogating, Comparing, and Reconstructing Mission in a Global Era,* ed. Lalsangkima Pachuau and Max L. Stackhouse (Delhi: ISPCK, 2007), pp. 3-25.

us of the importance of respecting the freedom and culturally distinctive responses of others. *Missio Dei* reminds me to include the distinctive responses of those with ASD or Down syndrome in my articulation of the faith. Our congregations need to be more attuned to the intuitive ways in which many adolescents with developmental disabilities encounter God at work in our midst. Finally, Guder suggests that *missio Dei* highlights the importance of cultural pluralism, boundary crossing, and edifying confrontation. Applying Guder's insights to ministry with adolescents with disabilities, we are reminded that we need to appreciate their differences, be boundary breakers by placing ourselves where we can share life together, and share with them an affirming presence.

When we appropriate the insights of *missio Dei* theology, we will find that we contribute to the expansion of the gospel. I don't mean simply that more people will hear about it. I mean that the gospel will be expanded into its fullness as we amplify the witness of our friends with special needs. For example, following the insights of mission scholar Lamin Sanneh, the event of Pentecost demonstrates that the gospel theologically enfranchises cultures by giving them a confession of the faith in their own language or vernacular. Sanneh promotes the thesis that Christianity, from the beginning, is a religion that expanded by crossing frontiers.

In order to cross the Jewish/Gentile frontier the proponents of Christianity had to relativize and retain certain aspects of its Jewish roots and de-stigmatize and adopt certain aspects of Gentile culture. The crossing of the Jewish/Gentile frontier becomes paradigmatic for all future efforts at conversion and Christianization. It is always the case that the sending culture must be relativized as the message of the gospel is proclaimed. By focusing on the indigenous appropriation of the message instead of the missionary who "brought it," the receiving culture is not only de-stigmatized, it is revitalized, paving the way for an authentic reception of the message and, therefore, a genuine conversion. The new perspective on the fullness of the gospel that results from a new cultural expression of the gospel can challenge and be challenged by other expressions and articulations of the gospel.[4]

From the perspective of ministry with adolescents with develop-

---

4. Lamin O. Sanneh, *Translating the Message: The Missionary Impact on Culture*, American Society of Missiology Series, no. 13 (Maryknoll, NY: Orbis, 1989).

mental disabilities, our job is to relativize expressions of discipleship that are too dependent on cognitive and psychosocial capacities that many of our friends lack and de-stigmatize their intuitive and holistic responses to the gospel. When we do this we will be participating more fully in our calling as a church to bear the witness of the Spirit. Guder has stated, "Mission is to be a continuing process of translation and witness, whereby the evangelist and the mission community will be confronted again and again by the gospel as it is translated, heard, and responded to, and will thus experience ongoing conversion while serving as witness."[5] Sanneh and Guder challenge the church to consider questions like, how will including adolescents with developmental disabilities in our community of faith transform our understanding of that to which we bear witness? My attempt to translate the gospel into terms that Nathan understands has certainly challenged my understanding of God at work in the world.

Witness

Professor Nathan

What better way to teach seminary students about nurturing child and adolescent spirituality among adolescents with developmental disabilities than to have a kid with Asperger's syndrome as the guest lecturer? I knew it would not be easy, though. For example, if you want to have a deep and somewhat sequential conversation with Nathan, you will need to have that conversation while you are assembling a complex puzzle together. The activity occupies one part of his mind and frees others up so that he can engage you.[6] I'm thinking of the time that Nathan came over to my house and we were praying before sharing a meal together. Nathan, whose family attends a Catholic Church, made the

---

5. Darrell L. Guder, *The Continuing Conversion of the Church* (Grand Rapids: Eerdmans, 2000), p. 69.

6. Rosalind Picard is developing technological tools that can "bridge the chasm between internal feelings and external display." She explains the difficulties in gauging the emotional temperature of persons with autism and describes how, according to her research, their repetitive motions can actually function to calm the autonomic nervous system. Rosalind P. Picard, "Future Affective Technology for Autism and Emotion Communication," *Philosophical Transactions of the Royal Society B* 364 (2009): 3576.

sign of the cross. I asked him about it and he admitted that he did not know what it meant. Nathan wanted to know why people in his church tradition make the sign of the cross, so as soon as he arrived home he asked his mother about it and they had a great spiritual conversation. His mother related another story to me. On one occasion when Nathan went to church the priest was shaking holy water on the congregation. When the priest approached, many people around them seemed to find this the ideal time to tie their shoe or put a hymnal down — after all, it is uncomfortable getting sprinkled with water and inconvenient getting specks of water on one's glasses. Nathan, however, raised his face to heaven and spread his arms. He did not completely understand what was going on, but he wanted to get as much of what he understood to be "good" on him as he could.

I once had Nathan draw me a picture of friendship. He is a very fine artist who, as a result of his Asperger's, is able to focus on a project and give attention to detail in a way that very few can. At first, however, I was a little disappointed with his picture. To me it looked like two people shaking hands. Had I been more attentive to the details, though, I would have noticed that the hands were facing the same direction — not the brokering of a deal or a salutary greeting, but instead one is grasping the other in a supportive fashion.

Nathan had already taught me so much and was very excited to support me by helping me teach my class. During the hour ride to campus we had a great conversation in which I prepared him to meet the class. When we arrived at the basement classroom the class was welcoming. Nathan was impressed and very engaged by a *Godly Play* presentation, involving props and storytelling, by a couple of the students. At one point he became extremely distracted by a piece of string, but he recovered. When it was his turn to take over I had not so much as introduced him when he marched to the front of the class, pretended to tap on the podium with an imaginary ruler, and said, "Professor Nathan, at your service." His first question was, "Do you guys know what friendship is?" His second question, to the students at this Presbyterian seminary, was, "How many of you here are Catholic?" When no one answered affirmatively, he proceeded to ask each of the eighteen students their denominational background. But what Nathan did most effectively was help our class understand that there are different ways of receiving and processing the information that constantly bombards us, some of which we are barely attuned to. Spending time with

Nathan and attending to his perceptions opens me up to God at work in a world of senses, sights, and sounds that rarely imposes itself upon me. In this way, Nathan is affirmed in his value by our friendship and I am given a broader understanding of the gospel.

Gibson has taught me about the importance of the diversity of the gifts of the Spirit. He can often provide comfort to his peers that I cannot. I need Gibson. James is not restricted by the conventions of corporate prayer, so he is comfortable making sure he has all of the facts correct when he is praying. He will stop mid-prayer for a clarification, with no damage to his own sense of spirituality. He has an admirable lack of self-consciousness in prayer that is quite healthy. I need James. Daniel vigorously plays his model monster truck, Grave Digger, like a trumpet when I lead worship songs. He has a difficult time singing, so this is one way that he can be engaged — he is not being a jester; he is offering a gesture of worship like David dancing before the ark. I need Daniel. They all bear witness to God's economy, which says, "Let not the wise man . . ." And they need my gifts and me as well. As Brett Webb-Mitchell has affirmed, "The good news is that these gestures are sometimes performed for each other — in the name of another or Christ — and sometimes they are performed by another person when we are incapable of the gesture. Why do we perform gestures for others and let them perform gestures in our name? Because we are Christ's body."[7] This is a nice way to explain what amplifying the witness of another is.

Iconic Witness

In the Orthodox tradition, icons are religious images (depicting holy objects, scenes, saints, the Virgin, or even Jesus) to which veneration is offered. To Protestants these images often look strange, never really penetrating to three dimensions. Unlike Rome's sacred art, the icon does little to reflect the historical period or the personality of the artist. While Roman icons develop and change in style from Romanesque to Gothic, Renaissance to Baroque, the Orthodox iconographers attempt to submit themselves before the personality represented in the icon. They are passing on a tradition, not trying to present physical

---

7. Brett Webb-Mitchell, *Christly Gestures* (Grand Rapids: Eerdmans, 2003), p. 114.

beauty as much as they are attempting to "express visually theological truths and to incarnate a spiritual presence."[8]

Icons provide a window into the history and theology of the Orthodox Church. But according to the Orthodox, they have the potential to open us up to much more. Orthodox priest and professor of dogmatic theology Boris Bobrinskoy describes icons as "a portal open to the glory and beauty promised to us, a grandeur and beauty of which we receive a foretaste within the living experience of the church."[9] According to artist Egon Sendler, "The icon is intended to be an image of the invisible and even the presence of the Invisible One." The icon is not to be reduced to a souvenir that jogs one's memory; rather, the icon "becomes a link between the person represented and the person looking at the image."[10] Sendler explains further, "[I]n the icon we see a divine reality which goes beyond the dimensions of this earthly world but which at the same time respects this earthly world because it is created by God to become transfigured in his Spirit."[11] Russian Orthodox theologian Sergei Bulgakov argued that the "sacramental dimension of the icon is found not in its artistic expression but in the 'consecration that gives it its peculiar power to communicate with the beholder.'"[12] The icon, in this sense, serves as a window into the kingdom of heaven.

The iconographer must remain faithful, therefore, to the sacred prototype. Each line, color, gesture, facial feature, and symbol has a fixed meaning. These narrow parameters are not meant to be a prison for the iconographer, but are instead the canons that govern the practice. Iconographers are defenders of orthodoxy, ensuring the authentic representation and communication of the faith as it has been preserved in the church's living memory. They call all of God's creation to participate in the act of witness: "The materials used for making an icon are respected as God created them to be used from the mineral, plant or organic world. They too are called to participate in the transfiguration of

8. Michel Quenot, *The Icon: Window on the Kingdom* (Crestwood, NY: St. Vladimir's Seminary Press, 1971), p. 93.

9. Bobrinskoy quoted in Quenot, *The Icon*, p. 7.

10. Egon Sendler, *The Icon: Image of the Invisible: Elements of Theology, Aesthetics, and Technique* (Redondo Beach, CA: Oakwood, 1988), p. 39.

11. Sendler, *The Icon*, p. 182.

12. Quoted in Eric Lionel Mascall, *Theology and Images* (London: Mowbray, 1963), p. 43.

the cosmos, since the task of the iconographer is to spiritualize even our tangible reality."[13] John Meyendorff adds, "By sanctifying water, food, and plants, as well as the results of man's own creativity, such as works of art or technology . . . the Church replaces them all in their true relation, not only to God, but also to man, who is God's image."[14]

A theology of the icon could certainly inform our understanding of the image of God and rescue it from being dominated by notions of rationality. The power of the icon's witness comes from the Spirit of God and from its various elements being re-placed in right relation with God. If God is our iconographer, then each person with their unique lines, textures, gestures, colors, capacities, and impairments, when called to the service of the Spirit, is able to contribute to the iconic witness of the church. The iconic witness is more about the power of the Spirit and strategic re-placement than it is about rational capacity, purposive agency, moral responsibility, or a capacity for creativity. This is true for people with and without developmental disabilities. The only way that adolescents with developmental disabilities who are part of the body of Christ can fail to offer their contribution to the iconic witness of the church is if they are not afforded a place within our congregations. Their absence from our congregations diminishes the fitness of our witness.

Evocative Witness

To evoke is to elicit responses or feelings in another or to incite one to do something in response to (often unwelcomed) feelings or emotions. My experience with adolescents with developmental disabilities, especially those with more profound disabilities, has led me to believe that they have a special evocative witness. Their presence and way of being in the world challenge at a fundamental level our theology and practice of faith. The presence of adolescents with developmental disabilities in my life has awakened my understanding of our interdependence as humans, has challenged my understanding of faith, discipleship, and evangelism, has caused me to rewrite my dissertation, has guided my

13. Quenot, *The Icon,* p. 83.

14. John Meyendorff, *Byzantine Theology* (New York: Fordham University Press, 1974), p. 135.

vocational decisions, has reoriented our family's priorities, has impacted the way we organize our house, and has reformed my understanding of friendship.

Christopher de Vinck in *Power of the Powerless* describes his brother as "on his back in bed for thirty-two years, in the same corner of his room, under the same window, beside the same yellow walls. He was blind, mute. His legs were twisted. He didn't have the strength to lift his head or the intelligence to learn anything."[15] Yet de Vinck notes that profoundly disabled people, like his brother, have the evocative power to influence action in others. Though he could not respond in any meaningful way, his brother had the power to move other people. In order for congregations to be impacted by the lives of adolescents with developmental disabilities, we must not have forays into their lives in such a way that our lives remain untouched. My point is that even those with profound developmental disabilities, who appear to have no capacity for purposive agency or self-determination, can participate in the congregation's calling to bear witness to the kingdom of heaven if we only allow them a place to appear.

The Witness of All Creation

It would have been easier to send Warren home from the *Ride N Romp,* our annual camping/therapeutic riding competition weekend. Not only was this trip the first time he had ever been away from home without his parents, his dad had recently returned from the hospital after open-heart surgery. Warren sang songs like "I Belong in Williamsburg" and urged repeatedly, "My mom is worried about me." When anyone tried to console him, Warren gathered his special things (an iPod Shuffle, a wallet, a small stuffed zebra, and some other items) close to his body and offered a posture that screamed "Leave me alone!" Friday evening his buddy came to me and shared that Warren had been sitting cross-legged in the shower weeping for twenty minutes while warm water washed over him. I was able to get him out of the shower and dressed, but I couldn't do anything to calm him down. He refused to eat anything for what was now his second meal with us.

15. Christopher de Vinck, *Power of the Powerless: A Brother's Legacy of Love* (Grand Rapids: Zondervan, 1995), pp. 27-28.

Saturday morning, out of concern for him and personal exasperation, I called his mother. I had never sent a camper home, but Warren was so miserable, and the time and resources it took to keep him occupied (forget engaged) were putting a strain on the entire group. After a frank discussion with his mother, we decided that we would wait until after the horse show to make any decision. That was a providential decision.

We never expected Warren to get on Bonnie (the horse). We certainly never expected him to win second place in his riding class. We never believed that an animal would be able to provide the comfort, familiarity, and sense of peace that we could not provide. As soon as Warren saw Bonnie, his body posture changed. No longer was he stiff, inward, and distant. Now, with Bonnie, Warren was open, warm, receptive, and relaxed. He stroked the horse's mane and spoke warmly to her.

After that experience, something changed in Warren. His key phrases changed from "My mom is worried about me" to "My parents will be so proud of me." He began to relate to others and join in the group activities. When one volunteer asked how Bonnie did in the competition, Warren answered unhesitatingly, "She was perfect!" On the bus ride home Warren never sat still — he constantly shifted himself in his seat in an effort to make eye contact with those around him. He even offered to share some of his special things with others.

The theme of the weekend was learning to trust. We tried to communicate trust in a number of ways, but God, as God has done in the past, bypassed our efforts and employed one of his quadrupeds. God always provides the resources and gifts for the ministry that your community is called to. In this case, teaching about trust was less about being creative and more about being responsive. God was there before us and was going to teach Warren and us about trust in a way we all could understand.

Friendship as a Missional Christian Practice

We live in a culture where the word "friend" can be used as a verb — I can "friend" you. I can pop into your life, as you have presented it online, and make comments that suggest we have interacted in a meaningful way and then disappear. This world of faces on screens has established a false sense of connection with others and a situation whereby I can devote myself to my friends in such a way that my life betrays no commitment to them. It is more important than ever that we recover the practice of Christian friendship.

To say that friendship is a Christian practice is to affirm that the way of friendship is a way of witnessing to the kingdom of God in the world; that through the practice of friendship we proclaim and perform God's redemptive presence for the world; that when we befriend another we are partnering with and fellowshiping with Christ; that Christian friendships create spaces in which God is palpably felt, works through us, and enables us to bear witness to the mysteries of God's redemptive presence. When we practice Christian friendship we are practicing witness.

Friendship, then, is a missional Christian practice that follows the example of Jesus, a friend of "tax-collectors and sinners" and lepers. In Jesus' world, like ours, people were being identified with their job, their moral condition, or their illness. How did Jesus liberate people from these perceptions and then restore them to community? Through the practice of friendship. Jürgen Moltmann's understanding of friendship follows his articulation of the missional identity of the church.[16] Friendship takes the general idea of love and embodies it. Friendship is the form that love takes.

Our friendships, like the church, can't be content to remain within one limited sphere of life, a very modern division created by Christendom in which the church supervises the religious sphere and is headed by certain religious authorities. Friendship follows the *missio Dei* into every sphere of living. Moltmann gives the following example: "By eating together with them [those on the margins] in celebration of the messianic feast he brings them the fellowship of God."[17] In the same way that the church is called to transgress boundaries, Christian friendship crosses the barriers of equality, rank, and social position. Understood within the larger framework of the practice of the faith, "Christian friendship cannot be lived in the inner circle of one's equals but only in open affection and public respect for other people. . . . The

16. "It is not that the church 'has' a mission, but the very reverse: that the mission of Christ creates its own church. Mission does not come from the church; it is from mission and in the light of mission that the church has to be understood." Jürgen Moltmann, *The Church in the Power of the Spirit: A Contribution to Messianic Ecclesiology* (Minneapolis: Fortress, 1993), p. 10.

17. Moltmann, *The Church in the Power of the Spirit,* p. 117.

friendship of Jesus cannot be lived and its friendliness cannot be disseminated when friendship is limited to people who are like ourselves and when it is narrowed down to private life."[18] This inclusive and transformative friendship is eccentric — it pushes beyond boundaries and offers life. As Christine Pohl has explained, "At the heart of mission is friendship. God's friendship is a gift available to anyone who is open to receiving it. It sustains us in mission as we introduce our friends to friendship with Jesus."[19]

As a Christian practice, friendship inheres goods that are accessible only through participation in the practice itself. As Reinders has phrased it, "[O]ne cannot reap the fruits of friendship if one's friendship is a means to another external goal. Friendship is its own reward."[20] Practices cannot manipulate God; God is unpredictable. Christian practices do not make God more predictable, but they do create spaces in which we tend to be more attentive to the unpredictable God.

Liz Carmichael, who has written extensively on the issue, offers what I consider a mission-informed understanding of Christian friendship. Friendship amplifies the missional purposes of a Christian practice in that "Christians have the essential counter-cultural calling to be friends on earth, to offer love which may be in the truest sense sacrificial, to build community, to be peacemakers and healers, to seek and promote compassion and justice, to walk with the oppressed and help their voice to be heard, to celebrate with all."[21] Like a good missional theology, Carmichael's understanding of friendship includes an ecumenical vision: "The praxis of friendship requires that in addition to forming friendships with the people close by, we should make efforts to cultivate a much wider network of deepening friendships in different continents and cultures, from which to gain understanding so that we may approach all people with respect and sensitivity."[22] As I have been arguing, this ecumenical vision also applies to including the

---

18. Moltmann, *The Church in the Power of the Spirit*, pp. 120-21.

19. Christopher L. Heuertz and Christine D. Pohl, *Friendship at the Margins: Discovering Mutuality in Service and Mission* (Downers Grove, IL: InterVarsity, 2010), p. 123.

20. Hans Reinders, *Receiving the Gift of Friendship: Profound Disability, Theological Anthropology, and Ethics* (Grand Rapids: Eerdmans, 2008), p. 349.

21. Liz Carmichael, *Friendship: Interpreting Christian Love* (London: T. & T. Clark, 2004), p. 197.

22. Carmichael, *Friendship*, p. 199.

underserved and marginalized within our own sphere of living. Friendship is a missional Christian practice.

As a missional Christian practice, the practice of friendship can be considered in Newbigin's terms as a sign, instrument, and foretaste of the kingdom of God.[23] Through the Christian practice of friendship we participate in the Spirit-filled witness of the congregation. The entire body of Christ, typically developing and developmentally disabled, has the capacity, grounded extrinsically in the power of the Spirit, to be signs, instruments, and foretaste of the kingdom.

As a sign of the kingdom, friendships that cross boundaries point to the God who took on flesh, the Son who was a marginal Jew raised far from the centers of religious and political power, and the messianic friendship of God with "tax-collectors and sinners." Friendships that cross boundaries are instruments of God's redemptive love, instruments of the kingdom — though it is important to stress again that friendship is not instrumental in the sense of being a tool to accomplish some other goal. The message and the method are congruent. As a foretaste of the kingdom, friendship involves both the self-revelation of the other and the sacramental presence of Jesus. In terms as strong as baptism or the Lord's Supper, Jesus makes clear that he is so closely identified with his people that "whatever you did for the least of one of these brothers of mine, you did for me" (Matt. 25:40).

23. This triad of sign, instrument, and foretaste, which became a common way for Newbigin to describe the church, was employed by him in one of its earliest forms in *The Household of God: Lectures on the Nature of the Church* (London: SCM, 1953).

chapter 5

Advocating an Approach

Opus Dei

> *"We will never believe that we have anything to give unless there is someone who is able to receive. Indeed, we discover our gifts in the eyes of the receiver."*
>
> Henri Nouwen, *Reaching Out*

Opus Dei

Don't be misled by Dan Brown novels or Catholic prelature; *Opus Dei* is the work of God. In *The Rule of St. Benedict*, *Opus Dei* is the Divine office, a way in which the day is ordered and time is sanctified in response to Psalm 119:164 ("Seven times a day I praise you").[1] *Opus Dei*, or the work of God, has been defined in the following way: "The term is used in the sense of work done for God. It is the public liturgical prayer of the Church distinct from the Eucharistic and Sacramental liturgies, through which the Church praises God and intercedes for the salvation of the world. Its purpose is the sanctification of the day through formal prayer at stated hours."[2] *Opus Dei* reminds us that the work and circumstances of everyday life are an opportunity to grow in our knowl-

---

1. Timothy Fry, ed., *The Rule of St. Benedict in English* (Collegeville, MN: Liturgical Press, 1982).

2. Albert J. Nevins, ed., *The Maryknoll Catholic Dictionary* (New York: Grosset & Dunlap, 1965), pp. 185-86.

edge of God and to participate in God's ongoing redemptive work. What follows is one approach to participating in the work of God, of sanctifying our spaces and gestures.[3]

What follows is not a prescription or model to impose upon your ministry setting, but an approach to ministry. Our ministry needs to awaken, or support, the religious imagination in all adolescents, those persons with disabilities and those without. We will need to be more attentive to our practice of the faith and the accompanying gestures: there is too much talking about God and not enough seeing, tasting, smelling, hearing, and feeling God. We need more images, different arrangements of space, stimulating smells, bodies in motion, the telling and enacting of stories, Christly gestures, embodied doctrine, and a world of tastes. How can our program of spiritual nurture connect with adolescents with developmental disabilities and offer them something that will endure even when they are elsewhere? How can we relate their church experience to their life experience?

When we choose adolescents with developmental disabilities as our friends and practice our faith with them, their evocative witness will challenge the way we understand discipleship. I came to the realization that if I can't teach prayer to adolescents with developmental disabilities, then I don't know enough about prayer. I need to rediscover prayer and come to understand it in a new way with their help. The problem is not that adolescents with developmental disabilities have cognitive impairments; the problem is a lack of imagination and an incomplete understanding of prayer on my part!

Below are six steps to remember when you are reorienting your ministry to include the gifts, contributions, perspectives, difficulties, and struggles that will accompany the full inclusion of adolescents with developmental disabilities in your community's witness.

Step One: You Have to Be a Professional

Despite what you may have read or heard in any other setting, the fact is that to effectively minister to and with kids with developmental dis-

---

3. By "sanctify" I mean that we set things apart for holy purpose. Our very lives are sanctified by the work of the Spirit; therefore we respond by setting them apart and offering our lives as living sacrifices (Rom. 12:1-2).

abilities you have to be a professional. Bill Gaventa challenges professional caregivers to recover the meaning of "profess-ional," which has less to do with a particular skill set or career path and more to do with "a declaration of one's faith and values," a sense of commitment, a recognition of gifts in service of God and community, and a discernment of the calling to stand with others.[4] It is this profession of calling to which I am referring. We are called to be professionals!

In order to establish a ministry that endures, you will need to partner with other "professionals." Identify who is working with and supporting adolescents with developmental disabilities in your community. Local Park and Recreation organizations might have Buddy sports programs; there might be a therapeutic equestrian center nearby.[5] Find out who is working with Special Olympics in your community; join them and help them be successful.[6] Win the trust of the community through faithful service. Familiarize yourself with various advocacy groups in your community and get involved. Finally, jump into the ongoing discussion about ministry and disability by reading books and journals and frequenting websites.[7]

Step Two: Develop Peer Buddies

Given our discussion of the importance of peer relationships in chapter three, it could be argued that the most important aspect of a ministry to adolescents with developmental disabilities is the development

4. Bill Gaventa, "Gift and Call: Recovering the Spiritual Foundations of Friendships," in *Friendships and Community Connections between People with and without Developmental Disabilities,* ed. Angela Novak Amado (Baltimore: Paul H. Brookes, 1993), pp. 55-57.

5. See www.pathintl.org (Professional Association of Therapeutic Horsemanship International).

6. See www.specialolympics.org.

7. One resource that is particularly helpful in this regard is Erik Carter's *Including People with Disabilities in Faith Communities: A Guide for Service Providers, Families, and Congregations* (Baltimore: Paul H. Brookes, 2007). Carter anticipates nearly every imaginable obstacle, challenge, objection, and barrier to the full participation of people with disabilities in faith communities, whether architectural, attitudinal, communicative, or programmatic. He also includes two very helpful appendices. The appendices include several pages listing websites that include the statements of faith of groups that address disability and inclusion and several pages of resources, in the form of book and article titles, accessibility guides, curricular resources, and organizations that could support inclusion efforts by families and congregations.

of a cadre of peer buddies who will share life with them. As studies have shown, peers have more of an impact than adults on their classmates, and according to Erik Carter the impact is reciprocal:

> Participating in extracurricular activities is both an enjoyable and memorable part of school and a valuable opportunity for students to form relationships, gain important skills, practice self-advocacy, and prepare for their future. Meaningful participation by students with disabilities also can change the perceptions and attitudes of other students, staff and the larger community.[8]

In our ministry, we have buddies (high school age volunteers) and volunteers (college students and adults). We work together to create an intergenerational community of witness. Volunteer/Buddy training consists in five major areas:

1. **"Am I making you uncomfortable?"** Galen may bound up to you like an effeminate gazelle, stop inappropriately close to your face with a little drool dripping from the corner of his bottom lip, and ask you, "Am I making you uncomfortable?" If it is your first time encountering Galen, the answer will certainly be Yes. Part of training volunteers is putting them in situations where they can learn to be comfortable being uncomfortable. If you can give them an idea ahead of time of the kinds of situations they might face, or even act them out, they will have a much easier time adjusting to such encounters.

2. **Affirming presence.** In order for buddies and volunteers to have any impact in the lives of adolescents with developmental disabilities, or to be impacted by them, buddies need to establish a presence in the lives of their friends with disabilities. This means going where they are. We encourage leaders and buddies to cheer for them at Buddy Ball or Special Olympics bowling (you will certainly stand out!); sit with them during lunch at school; trade text messages with those who are capable; take them with you when you run an errand; visit their home and let them show you

---

8. Erik W. Carter, Beth Swedeen, and Colleen K. Moss, "Supporting Extracurricular Involvement for Youth with Disabilities," *Exceptional Parent Magazine* (September 2009): 33.

their room; go to the movies together; or do a puzzle together. Faithfulness and presence will open the door to more meaningful interaction. Most importantly, we teach buddies and leaders how to be friends with adolescents with developmental disabilities. The program serves the relationships. Everything that follows about hospitable spaces, gestured practices, and proclamatory programs is intended to support the development of spiritual friendships.

3. **Creating hospitable spaces** in which the relationships between typically developing and developmentally disabled kids can flourish. (Step Three below)
4. Teaching buddies and leaders how to participate in a community of **gestured practices**, i.e., Christian discipleship. (Step Four below)
5. Developing a **proclamatory program** that speaks to the entire person so the buddies and their peers can experience faith together. (Step Five below)

Step Three: Make Hospitality the Context of All of Your Programs

> *"Hospitality, therefore, means primarily the creation of a free space where the stranger can enter and become a friend instead of an enemy. Hospitality is not to change people, but to offer them space where change can take place."*[9]

Hospitality is a Christian master practice that provides the context for ministry with adolescents with developmental disabilities. Christine Pohl argues that hospitality is not something to be handled by a "hospitality committee"; it is central to the meaning of the gospel. Hospitality involves a "closer alignment with the basic values of the Kingdom" and a "lens through which we can read and understand much of the gospel, and a practice by which we can welcome Jesus himself."[10]

9. Henri J. M. Nouwen, *Reaching Out: The Three Movements of the Spiritual Life* (New York: Doubleday, 1986), p. 71.

10. Christine D. Pohl, *Making Room: Recovering Hospitality as a Christian Tradition* (Grand Rapids: Eerdmans, 1999), p. 8.

Hospitality not only addresses physical needs (shelter, clothing, food) but, more importantly, it attends to deep and fundamental interpersonal needs like being recognized, feeling valued, and having a sense of being connected.[11] Practicing hospitality together opens congregations up to the countercultural and boundary-transgressing movement of the Spirit. When we welcome people who are marginalized we are participating in a foretaste of the welcome of God. The Great Banquet (Luke 14:15-24) that revealed God's universally inclusive welcome is the necessary context for the Christian practice of friendship to flourish.

The spaces created by hospitality are vital for the development of friendship. The same points Carter makes about school-day peer buddy systems, he makes about involvement in extracurricular activities: "Participating in extracurricular [nonacademic] activities can be a valuable way for students to develop peer relationships, gain leadership and communication skills, explore new interests, and experience a sense of belonging."[12] This is certainly true, if the activities are set up with adolescents with developmental disabilities in mind. Carter offers twenty strategies for increasing participation of adolescents with disabilities in organized extracurricular activities that are consistent with my approach to friendship and hospitality. They range from making sure students are aware of activities, inviting them to participate, allowing for choices, creating a welcoming atmosphere, making sure intentional support structures are in place, evaluating activities for inclusiveness, and giving kids with developmental disabilities opportunities to make contributions and to really participate with a "sense of belonging."

One of the ways our ministry creates space where peer relationships are developed and connections are made is through Student Leader Training (SLT). At least two Sunday evenings a month we gather together for SLT. SLT includes a broad range of activities including singing praise songs, having the kids bring in a picture that conveys friendship or forgiveness, making a thankful chain,[13] playing *Jenga* to

---

11. Pohl, *Making Room,* p. 31.

12. Carter et al., "Supporting Extracurricular Involvement," p. 32.

13. A thankful chain is made by cutting 8½″ × 2″ strips of construction paper and having kids write (or help them write) things they are thankful for on the paper. The paper is then made into a loop and stapled in place. The next loop is stapled through the previous loop, making a chain. The completed chain is taken home and families are encouraged to use the chain, tearing off one link per day, to pray together in preparation for Thanksgiving. The last chain is broken on Thanksgiving Day.

explain *ubuntu*,[14] playing musical food as a way of engaging the many smells and tastes of Scripture,[15] having an artist lead us in an artistic response to a Bible story, etc. Each semester we have a theme, one of the practices of the Christian faith, and all of the SLT meetings and the other events tie into that theme by means of gestured practices and a proclamatory program.

Step Four: Partake in Gestured Practices

Brett Webb-Mitchell is uniquely qualified to speak about the spiritual lives of children with disabilities. Besides his theological training and a Ph.D. in Special Education with a focus on religious education, he has been the Director of Religious Life at a children's center working with children with emotional, behavioral, and developmental disabilities. Webb-Mitchell argues that the curriculum for Christian education consists in passing on the gestures of Christ. In the performance of the gestures of Christ, he argues, we learn the virtues of the church. Therefore, the proper context for learning the gestures of Christ, one that is particularly accommodating to people with disabilities, is the body of Christ:

> And in this body, the Spirit of God does not choose to neglect or not be in the life of people whom the world calls disabled, let alone in the distribution of gifts, services, and talents in the body of Christ. None of the gifts of the Spirit are withheld or designated to

14. *Ubuntu* is Desmond Tutu's theological interpretation of the African philosophical concept that we are all connected. Tutu describes *ubuntu* in the following way: "'My humanity is caught up, is inextricably bound up in yours.' We belong to a bundle of life. We say, 'A person is a person through other persons.' It is not, 'I think therefore I am.' It says rather: 'I am human because I belong. I participate, I share'" (*No Future without Forgiveness* [New York: Doubleday, 1999], p. 31). Or, consider the explanation of African philosopher John Mbiti: "Whatever happens to the individual happens to the whole group, and whatever happens to the whole group happens to the individual. The individual can only say, 'I am because we are, since we are therefore I am'" (*African Religions and Philosophy*, 2nd rev. and enlarged ed. [Portsmouth, NH: Heinemann, 1990], p. 106).

15. Musical food is a game in which different food items are placed in plain brown paper bags and passed around, one at a time, one person at a time, to music. When the music stops, whoever is holding the bag has to take one bite of whatever is in the bag. Then the next bag enters the game.

people based upon one's academic pedigree, or an intelligence quotient score, social adaptation scale, or any other modern day assessment tool.[16]

What are gestures according to Webb-Mitchell? Webb-Mitchell uses the *New Oxford American Dictionary* definition to make the point that gestures are both static presentations and dynamic expressive movements. He argues that gestures are a kind of context-dependent "language" that is developed within a particular culture.[17] Like Christian practices, gestures are both universal yet with meanings that are nuanced locally. In summary, "A gesture is a fusion of mind, body, and spirit in Christ's one body. They are learned, practiced, and performed by members of Christ's body. The community of Christ is re-created by the gestures that embody the story of God's gospel."[18] I understand gestures to be an important component of Christian practices, especially with respect to ministering to and with people who find the "language" of gestures confusing due to a developmental disability.

Webb-Mitchell's theology of gestures issues in an interesting proposal: "Rather than making those with disabilities express their image of God in primarily a linguistic or verbal mode just like 'us,' the focus is shifted to encouraging both the able-bodied Christian educator and the participants to learn the logic, the grammar, that artistic mode of communication best suited for the person with a disabling condition via gestures."[19] Webb-Mitchell is careful to state: "A gesture is more than another way of saying 'body language,' such as a frown, a smile, shrugging shoulders, or pointing to an object; it is more than an accompaniment to a verbal cue. It is also more than symbolic representation, such as the Statue of Liberty holding high the torch of liberty."[20] Webb-Mitchell is correct: gestures *are* more than these things; however, gestures certainly include them.

For example, one of the central gestures of the Christian faith is

16. Brett Webb-Mitchell, "Educating Toward Full Inclusion in the Body of Christ: People with Disabilities Being Full Members of the Church," *Journal of Religion, Disability & Health* 14 (2010): 264.

17. Brett Webb-Mitchell, *Christly Gestures* (Grand Rapids: Eerdmans, 2003), p. 96.

18. Webb-Mitchell, "Educating Toward Full Inclusion," p. 266.

19. Brett Webb-Mitchell, *Unexpected Guests at God's Banquet: Welcoming People with Disabilities into the Church* (New York: Crossroad, 1994), p. 135.

20. Webb-Mitchell, *Christly Gestures,* p. 93.

to "cross" oneself in devotion. But the cross, itself, has a variety of different meanings. "Cross" has a formal dictionary meaning (an instrument of torture, a mark, two intersecting lines); a functional meaning (the sign of the cross, cross your heart, cross your fingers, an "x" that marks the spot); an affective meaning (How does the meaning of a cross differ between modern-day Christians versus first-century Romans? What is the motivating power of the true cross of Christ during the Crusades or a simple patch sewn onto a garment?); and a prototypical meaning (What criterion does one or a community use to determine what qualifies as a cross?). The community helps us to understand what the gesture of crossing oneself really means.

Beyond the words we choose, we communicate in a myriad of other ways. Say the phrase "What are you doing?" How can you use the same words with different intonations or physical expressions to communicate a very different meaning? When our gestures include words, those words are expressed with tempo, pitch, ar-tic-u-la-tion, and facial expressions that include the use of our eyes, forehead, cheeks, and mouth. Our gestures include oculesics (the use of our eyes). In gesturing, we might engage eye contact or seek avoidance of another's gaze because we are embarrassed, are stimulated, feel sorrow, have a desire to engage or disengage in conversation, or may simply need to look away in order to reduce the overwhelming stimuli from an emotional encounter.

Our gestures are embodied with kinesics (body motion). We employ emblems like thumbs up (or other particular fingers up), illustrators like talking hands, regulators like hushing with a finger to one's own lips or to the lips of a loved one, adapters like playing with one's own hair to release emotional energy, or affect displays like smiles or frowns. Our gestures are executed from a certain proximity — have you ever encountered a close talker? Gestures can be accompanied by physical touch or executed without. Sometimes gestures involve silence — at times, not saying anything and offering a nonanxious presence communicates more than any words could. In my estimation, gestures fit within the larger vision of Christian practices — practices are gestured.[21]

Since Christian practices are gestured, and our ministry model involves common participation in Christian practices, we need to be aware of how our friends with developmental disabilities might have

21. Much of the reflection above is inspired by Blaine Goss and Dan O'Hair, *Communicating in Interpersonal Relationships* (New York: Macmillan, 1988).

difficulties interpreting or participating in the gestured practices of our community. For example, many of my friends with ASD can't read faces, are extremely uncomfortable with eye contact, are hypersensitive to illustrators, and recoil from touch. Several of my friends with Asperger's syndrome don't understand personal space and are too busy with their own interests to engage the gesture the community is sharing. Creating the "space" necessary for them to be able to fully participate in a community's practice of prayer requires a proclamatory program that addresses the entire person.

Step Five: Develop a Proclamatory Program

The theological depths of Scripture and the complex intricacies of the liturgy are beyond the intellectual understanding of my friend Franklin, a young man with ASD (and, I must admit, beyond our understanding and that of most church leaders and parishioners as well). My theological training, while it has sufficiently prepared me to exegete Scripture and offer theological conjecture, has not prepared me to explain, legitimatize, or enter Franklin's faith world. John Swinton, speaking of his friend Steven, explains this dilemma: "My hopeless dependence on my intellect for making sense of the world actually prevents me from even beginning to understand how God might be present with him in any meaningful sense."[22] When we recognize that limitations in some capacities like verbal communication skills open up other avenues of discerning God's presence, then we might be more eager to engage other capacities for communing with God and others and for theological insight. We will become more attentive to our emotions, intuition, and feelings. With patience and imagination, and help from our friends, we can develop our capacity to communicate more holistically. If our intention is to nurture faith in all adolescents, then our approach will need to include a program of spiritual nurture in which the entirety of the program proclaims the gospel to the entire person. This may involve feeling faith, smelling sanctification and heavenly host(ing), as well as participating in the more traditional sacraments of baptism and the Lord's Supper together.

22. Swinton, "Building a Church for Strangers," *Journal of Religion, Disability & Health* 4, no. 4 (2001): 28.

Feeling Faith

How does one employ the approach described above in order to disciple persons with developmental disabilities in the way of faith and trust? Trust speaks to our interdependence. Faith challenges regnant cultural assumptions of the independent, autonomous individual as the highest goal of being. Even with the most intellectually capable adolescents, it should be clear that to communicate what faith and trust are we must move far beyond memorizing a few Bible verses. This is especially true when sharing life with adolescents with intellectual disabilities.

Trust was the theme of our Student Leader Training (SLT) last summer, and our setting for practicing trust was a therapeutic riding center. A typical SLT meeting began with buddies, students with developmental disabilities, and their families arriving for dinner. I brought the main course — usually donated by some supportive restaurant — and the kids and their families brought a side dish or dessert. After welcoming one another and catching up, we articulated in a prayer our trust in God to always provide for us. While we were finishing eating dinner we heard a Scripture story that offered a story about faith and trust and interpreted the story in terms of our shared experiences. Kids were encouraged to share with their friends, their buddies, or with the entire group, times when they learned to trust God or others. The very act of eating and sharing about oneself in community is an exercise in trust building — trusting one another with emotions, stories, secrets.

The mealtime was part of the program of nurture; however, it was through the horseback riding lessons that faith and trust were felt corporeally. In a therapeutic riding lesson, a student, who was not necessarily, or even usually, an experienced rider, learned to trust an instructor who challenged her to do things that were difficult for her. She learned to trust a horse leader who held the lead line and guided her through exercises that required core muscle strength, balance, and attention. She learned to trust side-walkers who escorted her throughout the lesson, attentive to every movement in case she should need their assistance. She learned to trust the horse, a massive and warm animal that had become her means of locomotion. And, finally, she learned to trust herself. Riders were not disabled riders; they were riders. And, riders grew in their competence on the horse, perhaps even having the opportunity to guide the animal with the use of reins. The riders practiced trust by playing games with their peers who were not riding.

Typical games required riders to trust their peers' directions or necessitated working as a team with a peer to complete some task. It is very simple to draw upon the full body experiences of trust and interpret them in light of our Bible lessons and our larger narrative of learning to trust God.

In this way, our times together practicing the faith had much in common with the fourth-century catechism as described by Hippolytus. Christian formation is vulgar, active, intrusive, and embodied. The full body and the entire community were engaged in discipleship. Many churches have traded gestured practices for memorizing some church history, reciting a creed, and affirming a few statements of faith. An explanation of the faith is not enough for Nathan.

The culmination of our semester of learning to trust was an annual event we call *Ride N Romp*, a fall weekend camp retreat that includes, for some, participation in the Therapeutic Riding of Virginia's (TRAV) Horse Show. Our activities included, of course, more riding, but also, at the camp where we were lodging, the opportunity to use a harness and carabiner to either climb a climbing tower or ride the *Screamer Swing*. I challenged everyone to attempt at least one of these challenge course elements, even if they only made it high enough to simply feel the support of the apparatus and the reassurance of the camp staff who belayed them. With the *Screamer Swing* as a backdrop, we connected the feelings they experienced to the biblical narrative. Later, the lesson was reinforced when everyone was given a carabiner as a tangible reminder of how it felt to trust. Because I had made this challenge, Nathan climbed halfway up the climbing wall despite a palpable fear of heights.

Later that evening, at our large group meeting, we were celebrating the TRAV show participants' riding accomplishments with a ribbon ceremony. Students' names were called, they received their ribbons before their peers, and everyone cheered. Nathan was not pleased that he had not reached his goal — a blue, first-place ribbon. He rode very well and received second place in a very competitive class of riders, but when asked how he liked his ribbon he responded curtly and with a sour face, "The color is fine. I like the color. It's what is written on it that I don't like!" Nathan was disengaged and sought isolation.

After our meeting had ended and the room had mostly cleared, Nathan reappeared. I found him at the ribbon box holding a blue ribbon — an extra blue ribbon with no designation had made its way back to camp with us. Nathan asked me if I liked his ribbon, and I took answering his question as an opportunity to have a discussion with him about being proud of your own accomplishments and satisfied with what you have received. Nathan interrupted my admonition to explain, "No, this ribbon isn't for riding. I got a first place in trust this weekend because I did the climbing wall and I'm learning to trust God." In the open space created by a weekend away together, in the hospitable setting created by loving buddies who have chosen Nathan as a friend, in the course of practicing our faith together, God taught Nathan and me about faith and trust.

Smelling Sanctification

How can we teach prayer in a way that engages the entire body? When prayer was our SLT semester theme, one way we practiced prayer together was to have buddies and their peers with developmental disabilities work together to make prayer beads anchored with crosses or angel charms. The ten beads could be shifted from one side of the bead chain to another and could represent people prayed for, times during the day that we pause to pray, or specific prayer concerns related to a particular issue. We didn't offer restrictive guidelines about how to use it — the point was that the prayer beads made it possible for students to take something that we did together at our meetings (prayer) in a tangible form (a beaded chain with a cross on it) into their homes and into the flow of their lives.

Following up on this lesson we wanted to stress that their prayers, represented in the beads, actually make it to God and that they, these kids, are part of a community of prayer that cares for them. Drawing on Psalm 141:2 ("May my prayer be as incense in your sight"), the Old Testament description of Moses' use of incense at the Tent of Meeting (Exodus 30), and a couple of passages from Revelation that connect incense to the prayers of the saints, I taught a lesson that affirmed the fact that their prayers make it to God and are pleasing to God.

While we were teaching about prayer, I lit a tea candle beneath a bowl of perfumed oil that, now heated, filled the room with sweet smells. Kids saw the smoke rise to the heavens and smelled the sweetness. Then I blew out the tea candle and held the bowl of prayer before them. I gave them each a bookmark-sized piece of cardstock with the verses we had reviewed printed on it along with this affirmation below the verses: "Let this smell remind you that your prayers reach God, and that other people care for you and are praying for you." Then, like communion by intinction, the kids brought their bookmarks up to the community's bowl of prayer and dipped the corner of their bookmark in the oil. The corner, now saturated, would hold the smell for a very long time and would serve as a reminder of both the effectiveness of their prayers and the fact that they are part of a community of prayer. Common elements had been sanctified in the service of the gospel. Sanctification can be smelled.

A full body experience of the faith is crucial for communicating to people with developmental disabilities. Consider the first-person account of Kathy Grant, a woman with ASD, specifically, Asperger's syndrome. I couldn't imagine her being moved by a way of teaching prayer that is not participatory — she was turned off by an evangelistic Christian service in which the pastor preached for over forty-five minutes. Importantly, Grant states,

> As a person with autism, the liturgy appealed to all my senses. For my eyes, there were icons of saints, the Theotokos and Jesus. For my nose, there was the incense that the priest used. For my ears, there was the music, because the entire service was sung. And for my mind, there was theology, history, and lives of saints, the Theotokos, the apostles, Jesus, and the Bible. I also like the vestment the priest wears.[23]

Heavenly Host(ing)

One semester our SLT theme was hospitality, and all of our meetings were structured in such a way as to emphasize embodied theological truths about hospitality. We shared many meals together and discussed what it felt like to be the outsider or stranger. We brought pictures that communicated "welcome" to us and shared them with one another. We considered the sounds, smells, and atmosphere of welcome and imagined how we might make our meetings a welcoming environment. Our

---

23. Kathy Lissner Grant, "My Story," *Focus on Autism and Other Developmental Disabilities* 15, no. 4 (Winter 2000): 245.

last event of the semester was a 50s Dance where our kids hosted the Arc of Greater Williamsburg, an organization that serves adults with intellectual disabilities. Our kids greeted them, made hors-d'oeuvres and served them, and sang a couple of songs related to hospitality. A young man with cerebral palsy and intellectual disabilities stood in front of the group of over 150, with his buddy, and shared what he had come to understand hospitality to mean over the course of our semester learning about it together. Certainly the atmosphere created by greeting, serving, sharing, and singing amplified his witness.

Baptism and the Lord's Supper

In congregational ministry, baptism and communion hold a special place as practices instituted by Jesus. In terms of the discussion on contemporary practices, these sacraments encompass in some way all of the other practices. They are "liturgical summation[s] of all the Christian practices," or practices in "crystalline form" that "ritually sketch the contours of a whole new life."[24] These two ecclesial, or churchly, practices also reveal much about how people with developmental disabilities are full members of the body of Christ and have the potential to call into question cultural suppositions about minimum requirements for being a full member of the church. As Webb-Mitchell has suggested, "Liturgy is a matter of significant actions that suggest meaning. Because it goes beyond intellect like speech and reading, liturgy impresses on the participants the importance of the inarticulate and that which is considered intuitive."[25]

With respect to baptism, Webb-Mitchell notes that one cannot baptize oneself; baptism is the act of the community to which we are called to be a part. What intellectual capacities are required to be baptized? In some traditions, infants are baptized with the belief that they will confirm the vows made on their behalf by parents or sponsors and congregation. In traditions that baptize based on a profession of faith, imagine how the community would be transformed if someone

24. Miroslav Volf and Dorothy Bass, *Practicing Theology: Beliefs and Practices in Christian Life* (Grand Rapids: Eerdmans, 2001), pp. 30-31.
25. Brett Webb-Mitchell, *Dancing with Disabilities: Opening the Church to All God's Children* (Cleveland: United Church Press 1996), p. 9.

with Down syndrome were baptized. In Webb-Mitchell's opinion, when people with mental retardation are baptized "the rationalist presumptions so prevalent in modernity concerning the Christian faith are undercut."[26]

For the parents of developmentally disabled children, baptism is an affirmation to them that they are not alone in raising their child — the body of Christ has Down syndrome, autism, and cerebral palsy. For the congregation, the baptism of a person with a physical or intellectual disability should serve as a reminder that any person who is baptized is not an independent individual responsible for nurturing his or her own faith alone — he or she is a part of a community.

Furthermore, baptism is ordination to ministry and, as such, is an affirmation that the baptized, regardless of intellectual capacity or developmental stage, have gifts of the Spirit to contribute to the ministry and witness of the congregation. A congregation that misses the fact that baptism is an ordination to ministry overlooks the particularity of the ordination of Jesus and the universal consequences of every Christian's baptism in him. In fact, the idea that baptism is one's ordination goes back to the church fathers[27] and has been developed more recently by Karl Barth, who suggested that all are ordained to the ministry of witness in baptism. Not all are called and gifted to become servant-leaders in the congregation, but all are ordained to the ministry of witness.

All members of the community receive gifts of the Holy Spirit for the building up of the community, as Karl Barth has suggested, and "all those baptised as Christians are *eo ipso* consecrated, ordained and dedicated to the ministry of the Church. *They cannot be consecrated, ordained, or dedicated a second, third or fourth time without devaluation of their baptism.*"[28] When our congregations baptize infants with disabilities and adolescents with physical and developmental disabilities, we make them full members of the congregation and we commit ourselves to

26. Webb-Mitchell, *Dancing with Disabilities,* p. 15.

27. E. Glenn Hinson, *The Evangelization of the Roman Empire: Identity and Adaptability* (Macon, GA: Mercer University Press, 1981). According to Hinson, baptism was a key point of reference for initiation and discipline. "Baptism, as some of the Fathers expressed it, was the layperson's ordination" (p. 73).

28. Karl Barth, *Church Dogmatics,* IV/4, Fragment: *The Doctrine of Reconciliation,* ed. G. W. Bromiley and T. F. Torrance (Edinburgh: T. & T. Clark, 1969), p. 201, emphasis mine.

discerning their spiritual gifts and providing them opportunities to use them.

With respect to the Lord's Supper, the image of the Great Banquet and the affirmation that this is the Lord's Table open it up to all Christ's disciples, who include tax collectors, sinners, seminarians, lawyers, and persons with disabilities. The important consideration about the table is whose table it is — that is what makes it so inclusive. Congregations often imagine that persons with developmental disabilities need to perceive things about the mystery of the Lord's Supper in order to participate, requirements we would never consider asking anyone else — they can't partake because they don't understand it. How much do I have to understand? What do I need to be able to articulate in order to partake of the Lord's Supper? If we baptize persons with developmental disabilities, then we will need to address any theological, doctrinal, or traditional barriers to their full inclusion. That might include asking some uncomfortable questions about how we organize for worship and mission.

Step Six: Challenge Church Structures

So far, this book has addressed the issue of how the church can overcome the various attitudinal, communication, liturgical, and theological barriers that make people with impairments dis-connected from full participation in our congregations. One of the greatest obstacles to the full participation of adolescents with developmental disabilities in our congregations is our inflexible, unaccommodating, sacrosanct church structures. Congregational structure or ordering should not be a monolithic template placed universally upon every community. The structure emerges from the response to the ongoing action of God in the world and the specific situation in which the community is strategically placed.[29] If we are to take the nearly 20 percent of adolescents who have developmental disabilities seriously, then we need to reform the way we organize ourselves for ministry and mission. Darrell Guder, who has served on PC-USA's General Assembly Mission Council's Re-Forming Ministry, explains:

29. Douglas John Hall, *Confessing the Faith: Christian Theology in a North American Context* (Minneapolis: Fortress Press, 1998), p. 192.

The church's task in every culture is to find the visible organizational form that is worthy of its calling to be the witness to Christ in that particular place. This is a process that demonstrates faithful response to the gospel, appropriation of the Spirit's empowering gifts for continuing ministry, and dynamic translation of the gospel into the structure and functions of the community. Wherever that empowered translation takes place, communities will confess our Lord and Savior Jesus Christ, practice his presence and rule in ways common to all Christians, and function as God's city on a hill, as salt, as leaven, and as light.[30]

The church needs to move beyond our culture's dominant evaluation of people with disabilities. When we consider Trey, for example, a learning disability is not "his" "problem." Only the community that denies Trey baptism can claim that the learning impairment is his alone and not the community's responsibility. Only the community that has given up on any tension between the gospel, church, and culture and unthinkingly follows the model of our unaccepting society will consider Trey's impairment a debilitating problem. Ostensibly "value-neutral" diagnostic indices that govern the way people relate to people with developmental disabilities have no place in our congregations and do not attend to the reality of one's spirituality.

The church has been slow to realize this and the consequence has been that people with disabilities have found our congregations inhospitable. If they can play according to our social rules, then they are welcomed. According to Swinton,

[f]rom the perspective of the church, such an understanding manifests itself in assumptions that its primary task in caring for Stephen is to find ways of enabling him to develop the necessary skills to be able to function in a non-disruptive manner with the structures of worship and fellowship as they stand at the moment. The task of the church is not to change or rethink its theology or practice in response to Stephen's needs, but simply to discover ways in which he can be made to fit within the church structures as they are at the moment. The problem is his, and the

30. Darrell Guder, "Missional Theology for a Missional Church," *Journal for Preachers* 22, no. 1 (1988): 232.

church seeks ways to respond to the immediate particularities of his difficulties.[31]

Accommodating people with developmental disabilities so they can be present in a nondisruptive way is not enough; we must challenge church structures.[32] We must be realistic about the structural changes that must attend becoming an inclusive church. It is a change from pulpit, to programs, to personal relationships (the changes must be at an individual and institutional level) that extend church beyond the walls of the building.[33] As Jeff McNair explains, "New structures would develop when the existing ones are no longer working. I would argue that if people with disabilities cannot be in the typical Bible study group, then the typical Bible study group is wrong. The person with the disability is not wrong, the structure, the 'way we have always done things' is all wrong."[34]

31. Swinton, "Building a Church for Strangers," pp. 41-42.

32. Beyond accommodation — "Changes in the practice of worship are not done simply to 'accommodate people with learning disabilities.' Such an approach begins with the assumption that Stephen is a stranger rather than a friend. We cannot truly be transformed if we assume that we are doing this for 'them.' We can only understand the need for change when we realize that we are making it in order that the Body of Christ can be made whole" (Swinton, "Building a Church for Strangers," p. 57).

33. "By basic structures, we mean everything from the architecture (steps, pews, baptistry), to the programs (classes, youth programs), to the service opportunities . . . to communication forms and social interactions (language, requisite social skills), to monetary demands, to group gatherings (worship services, social events), down to even rules of social engagement and the manner in which the church reflects society socially. How does the church need to change in its various structures (social and otherwise) in order to both facilitate and benefit from individuals with disabilities?" (Jeff McNair, "The Indispensable Nature of Persons with Intellectual Disabilities to the Church," *Journal of Religion, Disability, & Health* 12, no. 4 [2008]: 328).

34. Jeff McNair, *The Church and Disability: The weblog disabledChristianity* (Jeff McNair, 2009).

Taste and See That the Lord Is Good

Toward a Theology of Evangelism Informed by a Life Shared with Adolescents with Developmental Disabilities

"Thank You for Bringing Me into Your Life"

Heather's words, quoted above, have become very important to me and have informed the way I practice evangelism. I begin with the theological assumption that the life of God is ongoing — God's redemptive presence is always at work around us, Christ is always exercising his reign, his heavenly session. The Spirit is constantly calling people to repentance. At some point we recognize that, through the initiative and grace of God, we have been brought into the life of God. Our eyes have been opened so we can see what has always been around us. We now have a new take on life, circumstances, and relationships.

So often (in my circles, at any rate) evangelism is presented in terms of getting others to accept Jesus, to convince them of the benefits of letting Jesus into one's heart or committing one's life to Christ. The emphasis in such an approach to evangelism is on our action and our benefits. We find a spot in our busy life for Jesus (often hidden somewhere in our hearts) and add the ingredient of Jesus to our lives. To be brought into the life of God, on the other hand, is a more transformative, holistic, and comprehensive concept. It represents a total immersion, like baptism. We don't bring God into our life — we are brought into the life of God. This insight came from a girl who could not follow the evangelistic talk sequence at a summer camp. She did not understand that she was supposed to Admit she was a sinner, Believe Jesus died for her sins, and Commit her life to Jesus. She instead drew upon her experiences of the love of God, her experience of the practice of the Christian faith in a community, and the images from Scripture as it had been communicated to her; and she responded to God's pursuit of her in a very different manner than the one dictated.

The reality of Heather's response led me to ask, are intellectual affirmations the most distinctive feature of participation in the Body of Christ? In what ways does such a perspective marginalize those with intellectual challenges, like my friends with developmental disabilities? Hauerwas, who has been a faithful theological advocate on behalf of people with disabilities, has stated, "For what the mentally handicapped challenge the church to remember is that what saves is not our personal existential commitments, but being a member of a body constituted by practices more determinative than my 'personal' commitment."[1] This is certainly true, but I would add that we all respond within the limits of and to the full extent of our capacities. I have been led in my response to the gospel to pull together my thoughts and experiences in the service of the church by writing this book, a service that I hope has amplified the witness of my friends, like Heather. Franklin is still bouncing somewhere in affirmation of his being included. We both, Franklin and I, are responding within the limits and to the full extent of our capacities. We learn to love together and, since I am accepting a posture of discovering Christ in my relationships, I don't act as if I have all of the answers. There is no formula, no particular set of doctrines to affirm, no special set of statements to recite. There is a tasting and seeing that the Lord is good. There is a response to the initiative of God and a continuing conversion. This is evangelism on the way.

When evangelism is reduced to a program of the church, a method or a pattern of messages; when we overemphasize the "how" of evangelism and implement "effective strategies of evangelism," we tend to overlook the dynamic process of the witness of God. We are no longer surprised by how God works and we don't look for God's redeeming action outside of our message-delivery system. We also overlook the fact that evangelism should be directed to ourselves, as well.

---

1. Stanley Hauerwas, "The Church and the Mentally Handicapped: A Continuing Challenge to the Imagination," in *Critical Reflections on Stanley Hauerwas' Theology of Disability: Disabling Society, Enabling Theology*, ed. John Swinton (Binghamton, NY: Haworth Pastoral Press, 2004), p. 60.

The questions we need to ask of our evangelism are: In what way do we use language to proclaim the gospel in our ministry? How do we use language to interpret and explain the tasting, smelling, seeing, hearing, and feeling of the gospel? How can we be more attentive to intuitive ways of perceiving the gospel when cognitive approaches fail our friends and us? How can we offer them, and ourselves, more participatory ways of experiencing the things of Christ? *In this vision of ministry, verbal proclamation is part of the fabric of a proclamatory program of evangelism that is embodied through common participation in Christian practices.* How is the gospel inherent in the practices we share? What intellectual capacities are required to participate in hospitality, to be chosen as a friend, to be given thanks for, or to feel trust? The programs, and the relationships, are no longer possibly viewed as instrumental to some other goal (conversion identified as affirming a series of statements, decision for Christ validated by standing up at a "say so," or raising one's hand, etc.). Instead, the program and the relationships have a sacramental quality — they are places where we encounter the ongoing redemptive power of Jesus Christ through the Holy Spirit (usually through other people). I have not described evangelism with people with special needs; I have described evangelism as I have come to understand it. Thanks, Heather.

A Parable

On a certain day, a young lady with an intellectual disability was on a riverside beach with some friends celebrating the start of summer. She wore proudly a class ring. She didn't go to traditional school like some who were at the beach with her — she attended a learning center. But like all of her contemporaries, she had the desire to mark her achievements. She wanted all of her friends to know that she had a job at a theme park, that she had a school, that her academic achievements were to be celebrated in a goal-day ceremony, and that her hard work was represented in that ring. After playing a while on the sandy shores and in the shallow water she noticed that her ring had slipped off of her finger. Immediately she began to search for the ring.

A couple of friends who were around her joined her in her seeking. Those helping enlisted others until thirty people, kids with developmental disabilities, typically developing kids, college students, and adults, were all together on their hands and knees, combing the sand with their hands and filtering through the sand in the shallow areas of the river on her behalf. When the despondent young lady paused for a break and raised her head from her searching, she absorbed the magnitude of the search and realized that in pursuit of her ring she had found something much more valuable and meaningful than her ring. She had found something that she could share with others, something that could not be destroyed by rust and could not be stolen or lost. There was much joy in heaven over the search for the ring that was never found. What did she find?

Bibliography

Amado, Richard S. "Loneliness: Effects and Implications." In *Friendships and Community Connections between People with and without Developmental Disabilities,* ed. Angela Novak Amado, pp. 67-84. Baltimore: Paul H. Brookes, 1993.

Barth, Karl. *Church Dogmatics,* II/1: *The Doctrine of God,* ed. G. W. Bromiley and T. F. Torrance. Edinburgh: T. & T. Clark, 1957.

————. *Church Dogmatics,* IV/4, Fragment: *The Doctrine of Reconciliation,* ed. G. W. Bromiley and T. F. Torrance. Edinburgh: T. & T. Clark, 1969.

Bauminger, Nirit, et al. "Friendship in High-functioning Children with Autism Spectrum Disorder: Mixed and Non-mixed Dyads." *Journal of Autism and Developmental Disorders* 38 (2008): 1211-29.

Bigby, Christine. "Known Well by No-one: Trends in the Informal Social Networks of Middle-aged and Older People with Intellectual Disability Five Years after Moving to the Community." *Journal of Intellectual and Developmental Disability* 33, no. 2 (June 2008): 148-57.

Blanchett, Wanda J. "Telling It Like It Is: The Role of Race, Class, and Culture in the Perpetuation of Learning Disability as a Privileged Category for the White Middle Class." *Disability Studies Quarterly* 30, no. 2 (2010). Online at http://www.dsq-sds.org/article/view/1233, accessed December 31, 2010.

Block, Jennie Weiss. *Copious Hosting: A Theology of Access for People with Disabilities.* New York: Continuum, 2002.

Bosch, David J. *Transforming Mission: Paradigm Shifts in Theology of Mission.* American Society of Missiology Series, no. 16. Maryknoll, NY: Orbis, 1991.

Brooks, David. *The Social Animal: The Hidden Sources of Love, Character, and Achievement.* New York: Random House, 2011.

Brown, Janet L. "HIV/AIDS Alienation: Between Prejudice and Acceptance." Dissertation, University of Stellenbosch, 2004.

Buchanan, Michael T. "Learning beyond the Surface: Engaging the Cognitive, Affective and Spiritual Dimension within the Curriculum." *International Journal of Children's Spirituality* 13, no. 4 (November 2008): 309-32.

———. "The Spiritual Dimension of Curriculum Change." *International Journal of Children's Spirituality* 14, no. 4 (November 2009): 385-94.

Busch, Eberhard. "Karl Barth's Understanding of the Church as Witness." *Saint Luke's Journal of Theology* 33, no. 2 (March 1990): 87-101.

Carmichael, Liz. *Friendship: Interpreting Christian Love.* London: T. & T. Clark, 2004.

Carter, Craig. "Karl Barth's Revision of Protestant Ecclesiology." *Perspectives in Religious Studies* 22 (2001): 35-44.

Carter, Erik W. *Including People with Disabilities in Faith Communities: A Guide for Service Providers, Families, and Congregations.* Baltimore: Paul H. Brookes, 2007.

Carter, Erik W., et al. "High School Peer Buddies: A Win-Win Situation." *Teaching Exceptional Children* (September/October 2002): 16-21.

Carter, Erik W., and Craig H. Kennedy. "Promoting Access to the General Curriculum Using Peer Support Strategies." *Research and Practice for Persons with Severe Disabilities* 31, no. 4 (2006): 284-92.

Carter, Erik W., and Matthew J. Pesko. "Social Validity of Peer Interaction Intervention Strategies in High School Classrooms: Effectiveness, Feasibility, and Actual Use." *Exceptionality* 16 (2008): 156-73.

Carter, Erik W., Beth Swedeen, and Colleen K. Moss. "Supporting Extracurricular Involvement for Youth with Disabilities." *Exceptional Parent Magazine* (September 2009): 32-33.

Conner, Benjamin T. "Affirming Presence: Spiritual Life and Friendship with Adolescents with Developmental Disabilities." *International Journal of Children's Spirituality* 15, no. 4 (2010): 331-39.

———. *Practicing Witness: A Missional Vision of Christian Practices.* Grand Rapids: Eerdmans, 2011.

Côté, James E., and Anton L. Allahar. *Generation on Hold: Coming of Age in the Late Twentieth Century.* New York: New York University Press, 1994.

Cupit, C. Glenn. "The Marriage of Science and Spirit: Dynamic Systems Theory and the Development of Spirituality." *International Journal of Children's Spirituality* 12, no. 2 (August 2007): 105-16.

de Souza, Marian. "Editorial: Spirituality and Well Being." *International Journal of Children's Spirituality* 14, no. 3 (August 2009): 181-84.

de Vinck, Christopher. *Power of the Powerless: A Brother's Legacy of Love.* Grand Rapids: Zondervan, 1995.

Dean, Kenda C. *Practicing Passion: Youth and the Quest for a Passionate Church.* Grand Rapids: Eerdmans, 2004.

Demmons, Tracy. "Embodied Encounter Through Imagination and the Arts: Toward a (Barthian) Theology and Praxis of Pastoral Care and Counseling for Persons with Intellectual Disabilities." *Journal of Religion, Disability & Health* 12, no. 4 (2008): 365-35.

Doyle, Arthur Conan. "The Hound of the Baskervilles." In *The Complete Sherlock Holmes.* Vol. 1. New York: Barnes and Noble Classics, 2003.

Dunlap, Susan J. *Caring Cultures: How Congregations Respond to the Sick.* Waco, TX: Baylor University Press, 2009.

Dykstra, Craig R. *Growing in the Life of Faith: Education and Christian Practices.* 2nd ed. Louisville: Westminster/John Knox Press, 2005.

————. "Reconceiving Practice." In *Shifting Boundaries: Contextual Approaches to the Structure of Theological Education,* ed. Barbara G. Wheeler and Edward Farley, pp. 35-66. Louisville: Westminster/John Knox, 1991.

David Elkind. *All Grown Up and No Place to Go: Teenagers in Crisis.* New York: Addison-Wesley, 1984.

Erikson, Erik. *Identity, Youth and Crisis.* New York: W. W. Norton, 1968.

Estell, David B., Martin H. Jones, Ruth Pearl, and Richard van Acker. "Best Friendships of Students with and without Learning Disabilities across Late Elementary School." *Exceptional Children* 76, no. 1 (Fall 2009): 110-24.

Estell, David B., M. H. Jones, R. Pearl, R. van Acker, T. W. Farmer, and P. C. Rodkin. "Peer Groups, Popularity, and Social Preference: Trajectories of Social Functioning among Students with and without Learning Disabilities." *Journal of Learning Disabilities* 41 (2008): 5-14.

Farley, Edward. *Ecclesial Man: A Social Phenomenology of Faith and Reality.* Philadelphia: Fortress, 1975.

Fowler, James. *Stages of Faith: The Psychology of Human Development and the Quest for Meaning.* San Francisco: Harper & Row, 1981.

Fry, Timothy, ed. *The Rule of St. Benedict in English.* Collegeville, MN: Liturgical Press, 1982.

Fulkerson, Mary McClintock. "A Place to Appear: Ecclesiology as if Bodies Mattered." *Theology Today* 64 (2007): 159-71.

Gaventa, Bill. "Gift and Call: Recovering the Spiritual Foundations of Friendships." In *Friendships and Community Connections between People with and without Developmental Disabilities,* ed. Angela Novak Amado, pp. 41-66. Baltimore: Paul H. Brookes, 1993.

Goss, Blaine, and Dan O'Hair. *Communicating in Interpersonal Relationships.* New York: Macmillan, 1988.

Grant, Kathy Lissner. "My Story." *Focus on Autism and Other Developmental Disabilities* 15, no. 4 (Winter 2000): 243-45.

Greenfeld, Karl Taro. *Boy Alone: A Brother's Memoir.* New York: HarperCollins, 2009.

Groody, Daniel G. "Crossing the Divide: Foundations of a Theology of Migration and Refugees." *Theological Studies* 70 (2009): 638-67.

Groome, Thomas H. *Sharing Faith: A Comprehensive Approach to Religious Education and Pastoral Ministry: The Way of Shared Praxis.* San Francisco: Harper, 1991.

Guder, Darrell L. *Be My Witnesses.* Grand Rapids: Eerdmans, 1985.

————. *The Continuing Conversion of the Church.* Grand Rapids: Eerdmans, 2000.

————. "The Missio Dei: A Mission Theology after Christendom." In *News of Boundless Riches: Interrogating, Comparing, and Reconstructing Mission in a Global Era,* ed. Lalsangkima Pachuau and Max L. Stackhouse, pp. 3-25. Delhi: ISPCK, 2007.

————. "Missional Theology for a Missional Church." *Journal for Preachers* 22, no. 1 (1988): 3-11.

Hall, Douglas John. *Confessing the Faith: Christian Theology in a North American Context*. Minneapolis: Fortress Press, 1998.

Hauerwas, Stanley. "The Church and the Mentally Handicapped: A Continuing Challenge to the Imagination." In *Critical Reflections on Stanley Hauerwas' Theology of Disability: Disabling Society, Enabling Theology*, ed. John Swinton, pp. 53-62. Binghamton, NY: Haworth Pastoral Press, 2004.

————. *Suffering Presence: Theological Reflections on Medicine, the Mentally Handicapped, and the Church*. Notre Dame: University of Notre Dame Press, 1986.

————. "Suffering the Retarded: Should We Prevent Retardation?" in *Critical Reflections on Stanley Hauerwas' Theology of Disability: Disabling Society, Enabling Theology*, ed. John Swinton, pp. 87-106. Binghamton, NY: Haworth Pastoral Press, 2004.

Heuertz, Christopher L., and Christine D. Pohl. *Friendship at the Margins: Discovering Mutuality in Service and Mission*. Downers Grove, IL: InterVarsity, 2010.

Hine, Thomas. *The Rise and Fall of the American Teenager: A New History of the American Adolescent Experience*. New York: HarperCollins, 2000.

Hinson, E. Glenn. *The Evangelization of the Roman Empire: Identity and Adaptability*. Macon, GA: Mercer University Press, 1981.

Howe, Mark L., and Marc D. Lewis. "The Importance of Dynamic Systems Approaches for Understanding Development." *Developmental Review* 25 (2005): 247-51.

Kett, Joseph F. "Adolescence and Youth in Nineteenth-Century America." *Journal of Interdisciplinary History* 2, no. 2 (1971): 283-98.

Lewis, Marc D. "The Promise of Dynamic Systems Approaches for an Integrated Account of Human Development." *Child Development* 71, no. 1 (February 2000): 36-43.

Loder, James E. "Negation and Transformation: A Study in Theology and Human Development." In *Toward Moral and Religious Maturity: The First International Conference on Moral and Religious Development*, pp. 165-92. Morristown, NJ: Silver Burdett, 1980.

Lutfiyya, Zana Marie. "'A Feeling of Being Connected': Friendships between People with and without Learning Difficulties." *Disability, Handicap and Society* 6, no. 3 (1991): 233-45.

MacIntyre, Alasdair C. *After Virtue: A Study in Moral Theory*. 2nd ed. Notre Dame: University of Notre Dame Press, 1984.

Mascall, Eric Lionel. *Theology and Images*. London: Mowbray, 1963.

Mbiti, John. *African Religions and Philosophy*. 2nd rev. and enlarged ed. Portsmouth, NH: Heinemann, 1990.

McCormack, Bruce L. *Karl Barth's Critically Realistic Dialectical Theology: Its Genesis and Development 1909-1936*. Oxford: Clarendon Press, 2005.

McNair, Jeff. "The Indispensible Nature of Persons with Intellectual Disabilities to the Church." *Journal of Religion, Disability & Health* 12, no. 4 (2008): 321-29.

————. *The Church and Disability: The weblog disabledChristianity.* Jeff McNair, 2009.

Meyendorff, John. *Byzantine Theology.* New York: Fordham University Press, 1974.

Moltmann, Jürgen. *The Church in the Power of the Spirit: A Contribution to Messianic Ecclesiology.* Minneapolis: Fortress, 1993.

Nevins, Albert J., ed. *The Maryknoll Catholic Dictionary.* New York: Grosset & Dunlap, 1965.

Newbigin, Lesslie. *The Gospel in a Pluralist Society.* Grand Rapids: Eerdmans, 1989.

————. *The Household of God: Lectures on the Nature of the Church.* London: SCM, 1953.

————. *The Open Secret: An Introduction to the Theology of Mission.* Grand Rapids: Eerdmans, 1995.

Niskanen, Paul. "The Poetics of Adam: The Creation of אדם in the Image of אלהים." *Journal of Biblical Literature* 128, no. 3 (2009): 417-36.

Nouwen, Henri J. M. *Reaching Out: The Three Movements of the Spiritual Life.* New York: Image Books, 1986.

O'Brien, John, and Connie Lyle O'Brien. "Unlikely Alliances: Friendships and People with Developmental Disabilities." In *Friendships and Community Connections between People with and without Developmental Disabilities,* ed. Angela Novak Amado, pp. 9-39. Baltimore: Paul H. Brookes, 1993.

Osmer, Richard R., and Friedrich L. Schweitzer, eds. *Developing a Public Faith: New Directions in Practical Theology.* St. Louis: Chalice Press, 2003.

Overboe, James. "Disability and Genetics: Affirming the Bare Life (the State of Exception)." *Canadian Review of Sociology and Anthropology* 44, no. 2 (2007): 219-35.

Palmer, Parker J. *To Know as We Are Known: A Spirituality of Education.* San Francisco: Harper & Row, 1983.

Parker, J. G., and S. R. Asher. "Friendship and Friendship Quality in Middle Childhood: Links with Peer Group Acceptance and Feelings of Loneliness and Social Dissatisfaction." *Developmental Psychology* 29 (1993): 611-21.

Picard, Rosalind P. "Future Affective Technology for Autism and Emotion Communication." *Philosophical Transactions of the Royal Society B* 364 (2009): 3575-84.

Pohl, Christine D. *Making Room: Recovering Hospitality as a Christian Tradition.* Grand Rapids: Eerdmans, 1999.

Quenot, Michel. *The Icon: Window on the Kingdom.* Crestwood, NY: St. Vladimir's Seminary Press, 1971.

Reinders, Hans S. *Receiving the Gift of Friendship: Profound Disability, Theological Anthropology, and Ethics.* Grand Rapids: Eerdmans, 2008.

Root, Andrew. *Revisiting Relational Youth Ministry: From a Strategy of Influence to a Theology of Incarnation.* Downers Grove, IL: InterVarsity, 2007.

Sands, Paul. "The *Imago Dei* as Vocation." *Evangelical Quarterly* 82, no. 1 (2010): 28-41.

Sanneh, Lamin O. *Translating the Message: The Missionary Impact on Culture.* American Society of Missiology Series, no. 13. Maryknoll, NY: Orbis, 1989.

Santrock, John W. *Adolescence.* 10th ed. New York: McGraw-Hill, 2005.

Scheerenberger, R. C. *A History of Mental Retardation.* Baltimore: Paul H. Brookes, 1983.

Sendler, Egon. *The Icon: Image of the Invisible: Elements of Theology, Aesthetics, and Technique.* Redondo Beach, CA: Oakwood, 1988.

Smith, Christian. *Soul Searching: The Religious and Spiritual Lives of American Teenagers.* Oxford: Oxford University Press, 2005.

Solish, Abbie, Adrienne Perry, and Patricia Minnes. "Participation of Children with and without Disabilities in Social, Recreational and Leisure Activities." *Journal of Applied Research in Intellectual Disabilities* 23, no. 3 (May 2010): 226-36.

Swinton, John. "The Body of Christ Has Down's Syndrome: Theological Reflections on Vulnerability, Disability, and Graceful Communities." *Journal of Pastoral Theology* 13, no. 2 (Fall 2003): 66-78.

———. "Building a Church for Strangers." *Journal of Religion, Disability & Health* 4, no. 4 (2001): 25-63.

———. *Resurrecting the Person: Friendship and the Care of People with Mental Health Problems.* Nashville: Abingdon, 2000.

Swinton, John, and Esther McIntosh. "Persons in Relation: The Care of Persons with Learning Disabilities." *Theology Today* 57, no. 2 (2000): 175-84.

Tarakeshwar, Nalini, and Kenneth I. Pargament. "Religious Coping in Families of Children with Autism." *Focus on Autism and Other Developmental Disabilities* 16, no. 4 (Winter 2001): 247-60.

Tutu, Desmond. *No Future without Forgiveness.* New York: Doubleday, 1999.

Vogel, Jeannine, Edward A. Polloway, and J. David Smith. "Inclusion of People with Mental Retardation and Other Developmental Disabilities in Communities of Faith." *Mental Retardation* 44, no. 2 (April 2006): 100-111.

Volf, Miroslav. *Exclusion and Embrace: A Theological Exploration of Identity, Otherness, and Reconciliation.* Nashville: Abingdon, 1996.

Volf, Miroslav, and Dorothy C. Bass, eds. *Practicing Theology: Beliefs and Practices in Christian Life.* Grand Rapids: Eerdmans, 2001.

Ware, Timothy. *The Orthodox Church.* New York: Penguin Books, 1997.

Webb-Mitchell, Brett. *Christly Gestures.* Grand Rapids: Eerdmans, 2003.

———. *Dancing with Disabilities: Opening the Church to All God's Children.* Cleveland: United Church Press, 1996.

———. "Educating Toward Full Inclusion in the Body of Christ: People with Disabilities Being Full Members of the Church." *Journal of Religion, Disability & Health* 14 (2010): 256-68.

———. *God Plays Piano, Too: The Spiritual Lives of Disabled Children.* New York: Crossroad, 1993.

———. *Unexpected Guests at God's Banquet: Welcoming People with Disabilities into the Church.* New York: Crossroad, 1994.

Will, George F. "Will: The Attack on Kids with Down Syndrome." *Newsweek,* January 29, 2007. Archived from the original on May 17, 2007. Available at http://web.archive.org/web/20070516125514/http://www.msnbc.msn.com/id/16720750/site/newsweek.

Yong, Amos. *Theology and Down Syndrome: Reimagining Disability in Late Modernity.* Waco, TX: Baylor University Press, 2007.

Yust, Karen Marie. *Real Kids, Real Faith: Practices for Nurturing Children's Spiritual Lives.* San Francisco: Jossey-Bass, 2004.

Index